Other titles from Longman

On Becoming a Manager in Social Work edited by Barbara Hearn, Giles Darvill and Beth
  Morris
Quality Assurance for Social Care Agencies by Emlyn Cassam and Himu Gupta
Making the Best Use of Consultants by Philip Hope
Getting Started with NVQ: Tackling the Integrated Care Awards by Barry Meteyard
Caring in the Community: A Networking Approach to Community Partnership by Steve
  Trevillion
NSPCC: *Child Sexual Abuse: Listening, Hearing and Validating the Experiences of
  Children* by Corinne Wattam, John Hughes and Harry Blagg
NSPCC: *Listening to Children: The Professional Response to Hearing the Abused Child*
  edited by Anne Bannister, Kevin Barrett, and Eileen Shearer
NSPCC: *From Hearing to Healing: Working with the Aftermath of Child Sexual Abuse*
  edited by Anne Bannister
NSPCC: *Making a Case in Child Protection* by Corinne Wattam
NSPCC: *Key Issues in Child Protection for Health Visitors and Nurses* edited by
  Christopher Cloke and Jane Naish
Making Sense of the Children Act (2nd edition) by Nick Allen

Social Services Training Manuals

First Line Management: Staff by Kevin Ford and Sarah Hargreaves
Effective Use of Teambuilding by Alan Dearling
Manual on Elder Abuse by Chris Phillipson and Simon Biggs
Developing Training Skills by Tim Pickles and Howie Armstrong
Training for Mental Health by Thurstine Basset and Elaine Burrel
Monitoring and Evaluation in the Social Services by David and Suzanne Thorpe

Coping with violent behaviour – a handbook for Social Work staff

by
Eric R. Brady

Published by Longman Information and Reference,
Longman Group UK Ltd, 6th Floor, Westgate House, The High,
Harlow, Essex CM20 1YR, England and Associated Companies
throughout the world.

© Longman Group UK Ltd 1993

A catalogue record for this book is available from The British Library

ISBN 0-582-22566-3

Typeset by Anglia Photoset Ltd
34A St Botolphs Church Walk, St Botolphs Street
Colchester, Essex CO2 7EA
Printed and bound in Great Britain by
Biddles Ltd, Guildford and King's Lynn

Contents

Acknowledgements

I am indebted to many people for help, advice and sharing of experiences especially with chapter 6, 'The race factor in violence'. Mr N.S.P. Singham (formerly of the Race Advisory Group, Staffordshire Probation Service) and the several Tutors of Race Awareness courses I have attended were of particular help.

Mrs F. Kean made valued comments on Chapter 7, 'The gender factor in violence' and several colleagues in Social Service Departments gave me much information and help for Chapter 12 'Children and Young Peoples Homes'.

The publishers have been the greatest assistance in making this handbook more user-friendly.

I gratefully acknowledge the permission of the Controller of HMSO to quote some statistics and a section from the Report 'Children in Public Care' 1991.

I would also wish to thank many other colleagues who have shared their experiences of being victims of aggression and violence with me. And not least, many clients who have taught me much over the years – not always by methods I appreciated at the time!

Introduction

Any Agency, statutory or voluntary, that has staff dealing with potentially violent people has a responsibility to make their working environment as safe as it can possibly be. This principle applies to the Personal Services as much as it does to industry or commercial firms which have to make their working environments safe for staff and visitors from the potential hazards created by moving machinery or toxic substances.

The need to take more careful measures than was seen as necessary in the past has steadily become not only more apparent but more real for the Personal Services as society generally has become increasingly violent.

Though the increase in the 'violence against the person' statistics can be partly accounted for by an increased reporting of violence, especially in the area of domestic violence, there has undoubtedly been a steady and real increase over time.

Another disturbing aspect is that the level of violence used has become increasingly more vicious. The boot is put in more frequently by increasingly youthful offenders, even in what used to be called 'schoolboy fights'. Knives are carried for 'self protection' and used more often by all types of young men (more than young women) from all types of background. Handguns and shotguns are produced and used more frequently, not just as 'frighteners' in robberies but to wound, if not kill.

Laws are passed to restrict the availability of weapons and levels of punishment imposed by courts are increased, in spite of the popular myth that they are not. But these measures are proving to be ineffective. They do not deter those who are willing to carry and use as offensive weapons, instruments which have other and innocent uses, such as camping knives.

It is also impossible, of course, to find ways of eliminating fists and feet which also are used as weapons.

The bulk of the clients for the Personal Services come from this section of the community. They find their way, by various routes, into hospitals, Social Services departments, Probation Offices and Hostels, and the premises of the voluntary Agencies. It is because these Agencies share the same type of clients, sometimes the very same individuals, and share the same methods of working, that the safety principles that apply to one Agency are equally applicable to the others.

All the Personal Services interview clients in an office setting. Most also Home visit clients for a variety of reasons. Probation officers Home visit under the terms of a Probation Order or Parole Licence. Social workers will visit to investigate allegations of child abuse and make follow-up visits. DSS officers will visit to check financial matters, the NSPCC will visit for similar reasons to the Social Services. They will all make visits for other reasons as well.

So the potential for violence against staff in those Personal Services has increased, and, as far as can be seen, will almost inevitably continue to increase.

It is therefore necessary for the Personal Services Senior Management and Management Committees to take appropriate measures to ensure the safety of their staff. This is not just sound management. It is required under the provisions of the Health and Safety at Work Act 1974.

There are preventive measures that can be taken with regard to structure of buildings, interior fittings, alarm systems and office practices and policies which can reduce the potential for violence against staff. But in the handling of difficult and obstreperous people these measures can only go so far. It is inevitable that this type of client will come face-to-face with a worker, either at the office or in the client's home. Workers' professional skills are essential and fundamental to the calming of stressed clients, dealing with and helping to resolve those difficult personal interactions of the client-to-others and client-to-worker that are the essence of Social Work.

But, perhaps inevitably, the time comes when the best of preventive measures and the best skills of the worker prove to be ineffective with a particular client. And then violence erupts.

Guidance on what to do when that violence actually happens and how to cope with the psychological aftermath is as important as guidance on preventive measures – but too often is not addressed.

The primary purpose of this handbook is to give workers in the Personal Services some suggestions for practices and procedures that can be adopted to increase their safety while working with clients, some of whom can and will become aggressive and occasionally violent.

Managers and Senior Management will find that by adopting, and perhaps adapting them, to fit their particular Agency's working environment, an increased *feeling* of security will result which will help to provide the support the workers need in their day-to-day work.

Coping with violent behaviour developed out of two different courses I have run with a colleague for the Staffordshire Probation Service for several years; the first for staff of all grades, the second for managers focusing on their particular tasks. It can therefore be used to devise local courses, as an adjunct to courses, or as a focus for discussion at team meetings to help develop local safer practices.

Students may decide to adopt these safer practices from the outset of their careers and so not only have a useful time of service in helping their clients, but also a safe one.

1 Why be violent?

It is a human characteristic to become irritated, frustrated and angry at times in response to circumstances or personal interactions. But, in the main, comparatively few people vent that irritation, frustration and anger by becoming physically violent to another person. Most contain their feelings within themselves altogether or, at most, mutter a few well-chosen words under the breath or out loud. However, sometimes the last type of reaction mentioned can have a place on the continuum of violence, though at its lower end, if it is directed aggressively, personally and vindictively against a specific individual who is close enough to hear it, understand it and feel its intensity.

The things that anger people are common to everyone, although the anger-responses will vary to a greater or lesser degree (depending on the individual) whether they are a client, worker in the Personal Services or anyone else.

Common situations which engender anger include:

- Being kept waiting, apparently unreasonably, and without explanation – e.g. in a doctor's surgery, at a bank, post office or checkout queue in a supermarket. *Or* in a worker's waiting room
- Being treated unfairly in comparison with another person or other people – e.g. duty rotas, pay scales or promotion opportunities. *Or* between clients when they discover variations in the practical help (especially cash grants) they get when discussing their respective workers between themselves – something which is not infrequent among clients!

- Being refused something that is expected as one's entitlement – e.g. leave periods or 'perks of the job'. *Or* when the client is refused Social Security benefits
- Being treated rudely or off-handedly – e.g. in a bank, a doctor's surgery or by the worker's own line manager. *Or* when the client is treated that way by the worker or other members of staff
- Being given wrong information which then causes unnecessary problems and trouble – e.g. a bank, airline, or the worker's Administration Department. *Or* when the client is given incorrect information by the Worker or another Agency
- Being lied to
- Experiencing any or all of these things, not just once but repeatedly

If the morale and feeling of benevolence to the human race of the worker suffers when these things happen to him/her, especially if caused from situations within his/her own Agency, it is easy to recognise the greater effects on clients when they often have so much else to cope with in their daily lives whether seemingly or in reality? So should it cause any surprise that some clients, who may have had years of dealing with officials of all kinds and now see them all in the same light, come to the worker's office with their expectations coloured, perhaps with a weary resignation, perhaps by a simmering resentment? This attitude may not be specifically directed against the particular worker the client is due to meet, or even against that particular Agency, but is the product of all the client's previous encounters with other officials, other workers and other Agencies. And then the familiar 'Halo Effect' ensures that those same assumptions and expectations will be transferred to the new encounter.

And so the client, coming with all that 'baggage' may well over-react to an event or comment if it echoes an earlier bad experience.

The continuum of violence

A 'violent act' can lie anywhere along a continuum running from an angry and hostile glare (which in certain circumstances can cause a degree of alarm), through verbal abuse, a verbal threat, threatening gestures, a single blow, an attack causing minor injuries, an attack causing major injuries, to an attack causing death. At the light end it could be called, 'showing an aggressive attitude', towards the heavier end it becomes a serious criminal offence.

The victim or target of the violent act may be the worker him/herself or another person if the new encounter is a joint interview.

Alternatively, it may be that when the worker calls at the client's home several other people are present and violence is then used by the client on the others during the interview, caused not by any discussions with the worker but which relates to something that was said or done prior to the visit.

If a joint meeting was set-up by the worker to discuss a shared problem, e.g. marital difficulties, then his/her responsibility will be greater. If it was set-up by over-ruling the fear-induced reluctance of one of the parties and the violence erupts, the responsibility will be greater still.

In the last two situations the degree of responsibility lying on the worker will be felt not only by the worker him/herself but will be seen by his/her Line Manager and the Agency itself, should there be a subsequent enquiry at any level.

In Divorce Court Welfare work the courts now set an expectation on workers to encourage parents to arrive at an agreement over the care, custody of and access to the child/ren themselves rather than for the court to impose one. Their preference is to rubber-stamp an agreement. Of course, to arrive at an agreement really necessitates a joint interview at some time or other, even if the Divorce Court worker has to act as a mobile negotiator between the parties for a time. But where violence has been a factor in the marital breakdown, especially when there is a strong dispute over custody or access, the wife (for it is more often she than the husband) not uncommonly expresses anxiety about meeting the husband again. Often there is an obvious and considerable fear about it.

At such times the worker must pay heed to that anxiety. It may be exaggerated by the wife to influence the worker in her favour; it may be exaggerated because fear does grow with imagining; or it may be a very real fear based on hard and bitter experience. If the wife is pressured by the worker for the joint interview to take place, her expressed fears being over-ruled and the violence does erupt, inevitably there will be a series of questions from various quarters as to the worker's wisdom in setting up that joint interview. These will come from the worker's Line Manager, the Senior Management, very likely the wife's legal representative and possibly the court.

There are likely to be emotional repercussions on the worker as well as the actual victim, perhaps not the least being feelings of guilt for having been wrong and also for failing to have stopped the violence from happening at all.

If it is the worker him/herself who experiences any of the three types of violence (verbal, gestures or physical attack) the 'normal' feelings of being the victim of a violent crime will be as strong in the worker as for anyone else. (See chapter 6.)

Understanding the violent incident

When a client uses violence, wherever it is on the continuum, s/he has a reason for so doing, at that particular point of time, against that particular person. The actions are never *without purpose* even if they are *unreasonable* in the particular circumstances.

If the worker is able to deduce the *purpose* of the aggressive behaviour that the client has in mind, before it becomes overtly violent, counter-measures may be possible to divert the aggression from its climax of actual physical violence without giving in to that purpose e.g. handing over money.

There may be a single clear purpose or there may be a combination of purposes with varying degrees of priority or weighting.

Relieving frustrations

When a small child is frustrated s/he may cry, stamp his/her feet, throw a tantrum, throw an object (maybe a toy) or hit out at the person doing the frustrating. A key part of a child's maturation process is learning to control reactions to frustrations; being patient, tolerant and either resigned or determined to overcome these frustrations through other means. It is essential that s/he must learn never to react aggressively or violently to other people.

However, for a variety of reasons not everyone develops this capacity. Childish tantrums may still be thrown in adulthood and these can be very alarming to other people as they can result in damage to people or property.

Exerting pressure to get what is wanted

This purpose often occurs in tandem with point 1 above. For example, someone frustrates a desire and the subsequent tantrum is fuelled by a belief, possibly based on experience, that throwing a tantrum results in being given the desired objective. At other times it will be purely a planned strategy. This is how the Protection Racket works. But this principle operates right along the continuum, in all kinds of relationships, for all kinds of purposes, besides the purely monetary. It goes beyond the pressure of hard persuasion to become the pressure of threatened (either directly or by implication) or actual violence.

Dominating people or a situation

This can occur as a planned strategy in itself, when the sole purpose is to bully or it can be seen in tandem with point 2 above. It can be directed to one particular victim whom s/he terrorises or be a more generalised attitude towards everyone.

Case study

When working in a prison I met a man who was serving one of many short sentences for breaching a Court Injunction instructing him to keep away from his ex-wife. He cheerfully told me that he thought the repeated prison sentences were worthwhile because he enjoyed terrorising his ex-wife. By so doing he succeeded in dominating her life.

Punishing

It is possible to distinguish between two types of punishing behaviour:
The non-personal – for example, while denouncing something in general terms, e.g., 'all you Social Workers' or 'all you Probation Officers,' the sort of thing a drunken person might say when taking a wild sweep towards the worker. The intention is still to punish but it is more to punish the system than the worker who is seen by the drunk as representative of that system. The almost-accidental collision of the arm with the worker in making such a florid gesture does not fall into the category of individualised violence – but it can still be alarming, and painful.
The personal – a malevolent attack, purposely directed against a specific individual with the deliberate intention of causing fear, injury or death. An example is when a client adopts a programme of intimidation against a worker in retaliation for something s/he may or may not have done, or who has been chosen to be the representative of an organisation to be punished. It can also be a physical attack of a lesser or greater degree of seriousness.

Displacement

A weak person, wanting to show violence against a person or group of which s/he is basically afraid (e.g. the police) may switch that feeling of aggression to or physical attack on someone or something s/he feels can be dominated more easily and safely. A worker in the Personal Services may be seen as a 'softer' target who nevertheless represents an Agency close or analogous to the feared person or group, or the victim can be a person (say a partner or child). Even objects such as a shop window or the client's own furniture may be substitutes.

Understanding the aggressor

There are other factors which can help workers understand a violent

incident which relates to the aggressor him/herself and the arena of the
incident, rather than his/her more immediate and conscious decision
to be aggressive or violent in that particular situation.

Baseline behaviour

Every person has a style of behaviour that is 'normal', 'usual', or
'standard' for them. One person will usually be laid back in his/her
attitudes, another will be habitually edgy, another generally untrust-
ing and suspicious. One person will be verbally sharp but never more
than abrasive. Yet another will be aggressive and demanding and
readily flare into violence. Another will be a perpetual complainer and
seeker of support and yet another will exercise rigid self-control until
s/he suddenly explodes.

A knowledge of what style of behaviour is 'usual' for the particular
client will be of extreme importance in deciding between courses of
action should an 'unusual' situation arise.

Arousal situations

Whatever a person's Baseline behaviour, there are things that can
happen, the Arousal situations, which will move them from their
usual level of mood to another: e.g. from calmness to irritability, from
edginess to explosiveness. Depending on the person's Baseline
behaviour it will take a greater or lesser level of Arousal situation
stress to move a person on to a dangerous level. The Arousal situation
may well have nothing to do with the worker or Agency itself. It may
have happened before the client left home. For example s/he may have
had an argument with his/her partner or something may have
happened on the way to the worker's office. But equally, the client's
ire may have been roused by being kept waiting for a long time at the
office without being offered any reasonable explanation for any delay
– even if the delay involves the worker in a fraught situation with
another client.

The trigger

During the interview a trigger may cause violence to develop or,
occasionally, to erupt suddenly without any outward and obvious
warning signs.

A worker may also make a remark innocently that is emotionally
laden for the client and spark a reaction. But it is not inevitable that
that will result in a violent reaction. A worker would not be making
the comment with spite, as the wife in the case study clearly was.
If the emotion-level of the interview is kept low rather than being

allowed to run high, the client's reaction to any trigger will be shallower. A quick apology will disarm the situation. Indeed, the incident may well provide a focus for further work later one.

Case study

In a tense argument between a husband and wife (but with no direct evidence of pending violence beyond the fact that the husband invariably spoke in an aggressive manner), the wife suddenly snapped, 'You're just like your father you are!'

Her husband's reaction was an almost immediate and very hard slap across her face.

If the worker had not known about the earlier stormy relationship between the client and his father, and the hatred he had for him (of which the wife was fully aware of course) s/he would have been caught unawares by the effect of a remark that for most people would have been likely to have caused only some, and not violent reaction. However, in this incident it proved to be the trigger to a violent reaction.

The Weapon

At different points along the violence continuum different weapons will be used to cause hurt. These will range from hostile glares at the lighter end, through words, gestures, the use of fists or feet, an object being flung or swung, to a gun being fired in the physical violence.

The types of weapons at the heavy end vary from the more obvious ones that are habitually carried by some clients in the form of knives or knuckle-dusters to those that are only sometimes used, e.g. guns or gas canisters. Despite laws prohibiting their use many clients of the Personal Services still carry and sometimes use them.

Virtually everyone carries objects in the ordinary course of life that can be potential weapons; whether a bunch of keys, a few coins gripped between the fingers of a fist, a ballpoint pen to stab at the face, eyes or ears or hands, which can be severely damaged because of the tendons and thin bones. There is no sensible way to prohibit the misuse of those objects.

But there is one class of potential weapons that can be eliminated – those which are found in most workers office areas. It is not at all uncommon for workers to have a supply of articles which can cause harm; paper-knives, paper weights, heavy glass ashtrays, spikes, vases, mugs and staplers are the more obvious and common. Others include metal-cornered box files, decorative wall plates, metal waste-paper bins. All these have been used as weapons at some time or other, either in an office or in a home. Workers are well-advised to keep them out of reach of clients.

The Target

This is the person who becomes the subject of the attack; in police terms, 'the injured party', or 'the victim' more generally, if they are physically hurt.

The target may be the worker or another client in the same room. It is more likely than not to be the person who creates the trigger event by what s/he says or does, but there can be times when the person him/herself, by simply entering the room or being found in it, provides the trigger to that client. The anger and then the attack itself may be displaced from the real target onto someone or something else. It may take the form of kicking the desk, throwing something at the wall or slamming the door on his or her way out, any of which is preferable to an attack on a person, of course. But such displacement onto an object may not be the rule in these situations.

Each of these factors is crucial to the development of the violent situation. Removal of any one of the four (as Baseline behaviour does not alter in the short term though it is capable of change over longer periods) may reduce the level of violence used or prevent it altogether.

If the client has not endured already an Arousal situation before the interview s/he may be more able to cope with a trigger factor. The non-occurrence of a trigger may mean that though the interview may be tense it may not become violent. The worker, by ensuring there is no weaponry around and available for client use on the desk or elsewhere, may cause an incident to be less rather than more serious. The speedy removal of the potential Target as things begin to hot up may prevent a physical attack.

The timing of the client's decision to use violence will also lie somewhere on a continuum, from a point of long-term planning and the making of the necessary arrangements, through a decision to strike when going to the interview, to a near-instant snap decision. But that *decision* is still one that has to be made. People do not *have* to be violent. They can choose not to be so in relation to a particular incident even if they come under strong provocation. Though 'provocation' in various forms is frequently used and, at times, accepted as a defence in violence cases before the courts it is, at most, seen only as a mitigation rather than a total excuse. However, there has been a rare case of a jury acquitting a much-abused wife. But in that case, as in the others, the timing of the violence in relation to the 'provocation' is closely examined. And this is often the turning point on it being accepted or not.

2 Who will be violent?

Given the right circumstances, which will vary greatly from person to person, almost anyone is capable of being violent. Those circumstances for some, will be to defend themselves when attacked by instantly going into an attacking mode against the aggressor. Others will parry or take initial blows and only become attackers when, and if, the aggressor persists. Others again, will only become violent to protect from violence a more helpless person who is in their care, and for whom they are responsible. Those 'defending attacks' may only last as long as the initial aggression continues, and when that stops the defence stops.

Exceptions to this generalisation are perhaps those who are too frail physically to attack anyone (though such people can still be aggressive in manner, words and gestures), and those whose moral code precludes any and all violence even to the extent of rejecting violence to protect helpless people who are in their care from violence by other people.

Others again are only too ready to resort to degrees of violence immediately, right up to and including the heaviest end of the violence continuum.

The vital questions therefore are; who will be violent? and under what circumstances?

In chapter 1 reference was made to 'Baseline behaviour' – the style of behaviour that is 'normal', 'usual' or 'standard' for each individual.

Fundamental to assessing who may become aggressive and/or violent in an interview situation is possessing a knowledge of that client's Baseline behaviour.

Workers build-up that knowledge over a period of time, from their own contacts with their clients, usually in a variety of settings but most commonly in the office or in that client's home. There are other sources that should not be overlooked. These include any previous convictions or cautions the client has, especially for violence or drunk and disorderly offences. Notes in the Agency's records, other Agencies' knowledge and records, and information from the client's relatives, neighbours and associates are very important. While the latter groups may not be totally reliable (their comments may be exaggerated or minimised in the telling) it is unwise to dismiss them altogether. Prison Parole or Lifer records are of particular value, for these can cover a considerable period of time and show the behaviour of the client in a variety of settings, through a variety of people's eyes. These will include formal interviews by Probation Officers working in the prison, and probably other formal interviews by psychologists, psychiatrists and medical staff, works officers, education staff and prison officers. It is unlikely that such a constellation of observations will be available from any other single source. A caveat can be made that some of these may simply be a re-cycled version of earlier records in the file. While that is a possibility with some types of reports, the majority would perforce be independent of each other.

When referring to all records, note must be taken of their date. Assessments or descriptions of behaviour from years gone by may well no longer be relevant because, as already noted, Baseline behaviour is capable of changing, though this is usually over longer rather than shorter periods. However a style of behaviour that is consistent over a long period of time is highly significant.

Also a judgement needs to be made about both the accuracy and objectiveness of these records. Interpretations of attitudes and motives can be very wide of the mark especially if they are based on flimsy evidence and sometimes these are written as statements of fact rather than expressions of opinion. With the increasing moves to 'Open reporting' and 'Open recording' whereby clients can more readily see their records, they may become more objective. But there is the danger that instead they become more bland and so of less value in accurately assessing Baseline behaviour.

Taking all these together, a reasonably accurate and fair assessment of the client should be possible because s/he would have been observed behaving in certain ways in a variety of settings by a variety of people and in a variety of emotional situations.

This is fine with long-standing clients. However, there are greater problems with the first time visitor because there are no earlier observations to act as a guide.

The precursors to violence

The client's Baseline behaviour has its own origins from physical and psychological factors which have their own beginnings in either the recent or more distant past.

Physical factors

Physical disability.
There can be problems in addition to those caused by the disability itself. If there is chronic pain, patience with others is likely to be thin. Frustration at an inability to do the simple things that others find so easy can be intense. Especially when the able-bodied do not understand or even believe that the disabled person simply cannot do the things that are so simple for them to do. A car salesman made it very obvious to me that he just did not believe that I could not operate a gear lever with my semi-paralysed arm that he could operate with one finger.

A disabled person may become dependant, expecting everyone else, especially his/her prime carer, to sacrifice everything for his/her care. Some believe all Agencies should spring into action immediately to fulfil their wishes. Others may be less overtly demanding but instead adopt an air of patient martyrdom when they do not get their wishes, which can be both irritating and guilt-provoking to their carers.

Others, however, become fiercely independent, brusquely and even aggressively rejecting help even when they manifestly do need that help.

Case study
A client had gross speech impediments from birth. He had had other learning difficulties as well, but his parents had refused consistently the special education and treatment geared to his constellation of problems that were offered, instead insisting that he attend an ordinary secondary school from which he gained virtually nothing. Now, as an adult, he is usually remarkably patient with those trying to communicate with him but at times his frustrations do overcome him and then problems can arise.

This group includes those clients with speech and hearing difficulties which frustrates their ability to communicate. Few workers, except those whose work is specifically with such clients, know sign language, and not all clients can communicate in writing.

Head and brain injuries

A proportion of people who suffer such injuries at times develop new, often aggressive or violent, behaviour patterns. Sometimes the brain injuries are gross enough to cause observable trauma that can be detected on medical equipment. In these cases the origins of those behaviour changes are clear and can be confirmed. Although some injuries do not always show up using current technology friends and relatives of the sufferer still testify to changes in behaviour that date from the injury. As medical technology continues to develop that anecdotal evidence may be confirmed in increasing numbers of cases. Even when no such medical evidence appears, those accounts should not be discounted. But remember, an accident can be a convenient excuse to explain a loved-one's aggressive behaviour.

A slightly different factor which also arises from an injury is the psychological stress that can develop after an accident.

Organic trauma

Similar effects to those described above can develop from organic diseases that affect the brain. Trauma at certain locations, for example the effects of the tertiary stage of syphilis and sometimes epilepsy or Alzheimer's disease can also result in episodic aggression and even violence. Needless to say, those results do not occur with every sufferer from these diseases.

Alcohol and drugs

The effects of these on behaviour are well known and barely need reiteration. But with the advent of newer concentrations of drugs, for example crack, as well as the usual variations in the purity, or lack of it, of the common drugs, the effects on their users can be unpredictable. Also taking them in normal sized doses, but concentrated in a short period of time, mixing the drugs or mixing drugs and alcohol, further increases the unpredictability of their effects on the behaviour of their users. Even the users themselves cannot be certain of what effects will be experienced on every occasion, especially with some drugs such as LSD.

Hunger, cold, physical exhaustion

These physical factors are often overlooked because they are not so acute as those listed above. A client who has been waiting on the office doorstep from early in the morning after sleeping rough, is not likely to be in a suitable frame of mind or body for a deep casework discussion of his/her 'underlying problems'. The Salvation Army, from its beginning, adopted the tactic of 'feeding the body before saving the soul' and showed sound psychological sense in having that order of priorities. A mug of tea or coffee, some sandwiches, a warm bed and the opportunity of a wash will make a world of difference to the client's general outlook and to his/her attitude to the worker. It can even promote a greater willingness to work with the worker, albeit for the immediate future. The potentiality for violence will also be reduced.

There is, of course, the risk that many other clients in a similar state will be eagerly awaiting the arrival of the worker who 'feeds the body' the next morning!

Psychological factors

Physical factors can increase the potential for violent behaviour as they affect the psychological outlook, whether displayed by lack of patience, frustration, irritability, incomprehension or exhaustion. But there are other factors that are, more specifically and directly, psychological or psychiatric.

Mental illness
This generic term includes the schizophrenias, paranoia and depression. The first two, in particular, can affect the perception of the world by the patient through delusions or hallucinations. Personality disorders can be included, although a purist might consider that that ought to be put in a category on its own.

Learning difficulties (mental handicap)
This condition does not automatically mean the sufferer has a greater potential for violence. But such people may often find their world more confusing, bewildering and moving faster than they can cope with or can handle. When other people fail to understand this, and so fail to operate at a slower pace and capability, it is hardly surprising that frustration sometimes flashes out into the incomprehensible and uncomprehending world.

Upbringing
Everyone takes their norms of behaviour from their environment, which is then coloured by their own particular personality structure. These two factors can be described as the basic building materials for development. Adult norms are then developed from the child's earliest years, from their changing environments (e.g. brothers and sisters arriving in the household, school, meeting more people) which

are then continually modified by later environments and influences, developments and/or alterations in their personality structure, experiences they have and decisions they make about their ways of behaving (e.g. becoming dependant on drugs or alcohol, or on the other hand, attending Behaviour Modification courses).

These modifications to norms of behaviour usually happen over fairly long periods of time, though occasionally a dramatic or traumatic experience can occur that speeds up a change in those norms, so this does not contradict the earlier comments on 'Baseline behaviour' for that holds, certainly over the shorter periods of time.

So a child's upbringing, both in the verbalised rules laid down and more particularly by the norms of behaviour s/he sees, especially in the nuclear family, are of crucial importance to setting his/her own standards of behaviour. If aggressive behaviour and violence are a standard part of family life either between the parents or towards the children, it is hardly surprising that this behaviour is assumed by the children to be the normal or ordinary way to behave, and that it can often carry on from generation to generation.

The instant assessment

Usually the first person the client meets at the office is the receptionist. At that point of meeting, unspoken 'messages' pass between them, supplementing or even supplanting whatever words are actually used. The greeting can be welcoming, or the same welcoming words can be spoken with a tone and attitude that conveys the unspoken hostile message of, 'What are you coming here for, bothering me?'

The client, in asking for their worker, can show many different feelings, from resentment, irritation, hostility or aggression, anxiety or even desperation, or hope and confidence.

Prejudices can be silently telegraphed in both directions.

Of course, the client is likely to be far more ready to use words to convey what they feel, for there is an expectation that the receptionist will be verbally polite at the very least.

The receptionist's initial, quick assessment and description of the client's demeanour, manner of speech and approach can be of the utmost help to the worker when making his/her decision about the location of, and approach to, the interview.

On several occasions the receptionist's description of a casual caller, whether s/he is drunk and/or aggressive has caused me to decide to interview the caller in an otherwise empty waiting area rather than in an office past the security door. Also advance notice of a client's distress has caused me to interview him/her in a quiet room with a cup of coffee.

Of course part of that quick assessment will be the nature of the problem that the caller, especially a casual caller, has come to the Agency about in the first place, whether it is confrontational, emotional or a demand for money.

Quite clearly the receptionist's post is a key one that needs personal maturity, training and experience. But too often these responsibilities are pushed on to a young member of staff, or they are judged to be an adjunct to a secretarial or clerical job.

3 Preventing violence – the office

It has become increasingly clear to Agencies' senior management and management committees that measures need to be taken to prevent violence by clients to their workers.

To provide total safety for workers would inevitably preclude all the forms of contact with clients that show concern or a caring attitude to and for them. For total safety would require all interviews to be conducted through barriers stretching from floor to ceiling, with only a grill to speak through and perhaps a narrow slit for the passing of documents and a desk stretching right across the room dividing it in two. The clients' seats would be bolted to the floor. And there would be no Home visits at all.

Though there are offices where that kind of provision has been made, it is hardly conducive to the sharing of confidences in a caring personal relationship, which is what Social Work is all about.

So staff safety has to be balanced with caring client contact, and vice versa.

Though it is the Agency's Senior Management who carry the responsibility for providing a safe working environment, in the final analysis it should be the local office manager who does this balancing act, because each office situation is unique in its location, building structure, personnel and client types. There are obviously major differences between a small rural office and a multi-team inner city office.

This means that the office manager must be made aware of what the types of problems are that may be created by the structure of the building s/he is responsible for, if s/he is not only too well aware of them already, and in their existing security arrangements, of which s/he may not be aware and what security facilities are available. S/he then has to have a Senior Management who is prepared to listen, but if necessary to refine and improve, his/her recommendations – but in consultation throughout.

Case study
One area's Senior Administrative Management instructed a security company to install identical alarm systems throughout that Agency's offices without consulting any office manager or even informing them of what was being done! The security company's workmen simply arrived on office doorsteps announcing they were to install this particular type of alarm system, which incidentially was not a particularly suitable system for the type of Agency.

An existing building may well have aspects that are inherently unsafe for the use to which that building is currently being put and employing new safety measures can be costly. Bearing in mind budgetary constraints and other controls from Senior Management, the office manager will have to make a careful assessment of the existing working environment and the office working practices from the angle of staff safety, as well as client comfort and service delivery. Although the responsibility and the task is that of the office manager, workers of all grades should be involved in this assessment process. As they are the people who each day cope with the problems and stresses caused by the working environment, their input is invaluable to management in assessing overall changes. By listening to their views the management is showing that the voice of those at the sharp end can be heard. Too often, main-grade workers feel that as office managers are dealing with the actual clients less and less, they, together with Senior Management, are out of touch with the reality of present day Social Work.

Reception and Waiting Areas

Safety measures begin at Reception and the Waiting Area, whether that is a room, an open concourse or a corridor.

Does the receptionist work in a position that makes him/her vulnerable?

Case study
At one office the receptionist was located in the Waiting Area, sitting at a typewriter on a desk which had a heavy glass ashtray on it. Metal-cornered box files were scattered about. All the Social Work staff had offices on the other side of a door which had a digital lock and which was invariable shut and locked. Another was positioned at an open desk in the Waiting Area whilst the staff interviewed their clients in small offices opening off that area. It was those offices that had a barrier of polycarbonate to the ceiling, a grill to speak through, a desk from wall to wall, separate doors for the worker and client and an alarm button on the worker's side of the desk.

Another General Office had a door that opened directly into the Waiting Area and that door was kept permanently ajar except in the depths of winter, and then it was still unlocked. One day an extremely irate client stormed in who was drunk and had a history of psychiatric illness, slammed straight into the General Office. He repeatedly threatened to 'batter' the secretaries and the two Probation Officers who were in the General Office unless he got what he wanted immediately, before finally leaving, taking the two Probation Officers with him forcibly.

Had that door been shut and locked, the whole situation could have been more effectively controlled from its outset.

Positioning the receptionist behind a sliding hatch does not give automatic safety. A glass hatch can be smashed, scattering glass over the receptionist. Or s/he may be struck with a blow through the open hatch. But a wooden hatch is very unwelcoming and only solves part of the problem and is not a good balance between presenting a welcoming attitude to the client and safety of staff.

So a compromise needs to be worked out in relation to the structure, facilities and layout of the office. Because of the distinct differences between the jobs of the receptionist and that of workers in the Personal Services, there are measures that are appropriate for the former which would not be appropriate for the latter, i.e. the physical separation of the client from the receptionist is acceptable but the physical separation of client and worker would not be appropriate.

One system would be a sliding polycarbonate hatch (which is transparent but unbreakable) with a counter that is two-feet wide on the client side in the Waiting Area. The receptionist would sit two or three feet away from the hatch, which would still be within his/her reach but would put him/her almost entirely away from the danger of a blow.

In another office, because of local circumstances, it may be better to place the receptionist behind a polycarbonate screen, just too high for the client to reach over and with a six inch gap between the bottom edge of the screen and the counter top for any documents to be handed through. Conversation at normal tone levels is perfectly possible, the receptionist is safe and few clients are likely to be upset by it because the system is common enough in other places such as the reception at doctors' surgeries and post offices, and any betting shops they may go to.

The furniture in the Waiting Area will need to be reviewed. Fixed padded benches are safer than the more usual light-weight plastic chairs (they can't be flung or swung) but they are vulnerable to slashing by disgruntled clients or their waiting friends. While the damaged benches would not be dangerous, they look tatty and this does not present a good image of the Agency to new clients. They are also very expensive to keep repairing.

Most Waiting Areas provide ashtrays of some kind, realistically recognising that there are clients who will blithely ignore any 'No Smoking' signs, and is it worth making it a permanent confrontational issue? Make sure the ashtrays are of a kind that cannot be used or adapted for use as weapons.

A number of Waiting Areas have a metal box that has two sections sloping down to a gap in the middle for the cigarette ends and ash. With sharp points at each corner, light enough to swing or fling, these make ideal weapons. They are, however, heavy enough to cause severe wounds and permanent scarring, and perhaps crush an area of skull.

Metal waste paper bins, although they don't have sharp corners, can still be effective weapons.

A safe ashtray is the small, light type, made of foil. Though they are certain to be screwed up by some clients or to disappear, they are cheap to replace and totally useless as weapons. These should not be confused with a similar type, made of paper-thin metal which can easily be crushed into a rigid enough stabbing weapon for the eyes or into an edge of thin metal that can be used to slash a face. When tested, it took me just two minutes to make one into a stabbing point at one end and the edge for slashing at the other.

The building structure

Comparatively few offices in the Personal Services sector have been purpose-built and fewer still seem to have had staff safety and security considerations incorporated into their design even when they have been purpose-built.

The most basic security device is the lockable door between the public Waiting Area and the office part of the building – in which the Reception position should be included. Perhaps the best type of locks for this purpose are the digital ones that are opened by pressing buttons in a coded sequence. They vary in complexity and the code itself can easily be changed at intervals as some clients will learn the code for themselves by peering over the worker's shoulder while s/he operates it. Another type is operated by sliding a card with an electronically printed code down a slit. But then that means carrying yet another card and they tend to be larger than credit card size.

Corridors themselves can create a hazard. One hostel had an abrupt bend partway down a long first-floor corridor. It was possible for a resident to lurk there, unseen from down the corridor. In another office building, the corridor to an annex with four offices and the clients' toilet led through a heavy, virtually soundproof fire door that had to be kept permanently shut though not locked because of Fire Regulations. That effectively isolated the annex. It was not uncommon for only one of those offices to be occupied, which meant that the worker was vulnerable, not only from his/her own clients but from any other clients who needed to go through to the clients' toilet. In both buildings the problem was created by the structure itself. Eliminating the problem would therefore have required altering the structures themselves. This judged to be impossibly expensive in the latter case and logistically impossible in the former.

The risk factor was reduced, though not eliminated in the latter case, by changing office practices in regulating the number and type of clients that would be seen in those offices when a worker was necessarily alone there, and in the former example by placing a large mirror on the wall at an angle to reflect that corner down the corridor.

Furniture and fittings

The individual office layout itself can make for a safer or less safe working environment. Even in purpose-built offices there often seems to be some rooms left where the structure and size of the rooms themselves, and the position of the door in relation to those factors, is such that there is no furniture layout that can be considered safe – only that one layout might be a shade less precarious than another.

Apart from those factors, even in good-sized rooms it is not uncommon for a worker to quite happily wedge him/herself in behind a desk, flanked by a filing cabinet and the wastepaper basket and to position the client at the side of the desk, between themselves and the door. S/he will be equally likely to have a paper-knife and heavy glass ashtray on the desk with perhaps a mug and a stapler, and a plant or vase on the filing cabinet or window sill. This could be a dangerous situation if the client decides to become physical!

It has been said that heavy ashtrays, framed photographs, plants and vases on the desk and around the room help to create a relaxed interviewing atmosphere. It is perhaps possible they do, for the worker and for those clients who are sensitive to such things. But it is too late to try to get them out of the way if the client begins to become agitated. After all, these are just the things that some people throw at each other during family rows at home. It may look funny on a TV show but it is not so in real life.

There is some debate over who should have the most direct access to the door – the client who may want to storm out of the room in a temper or the worker who may need to escape for safety reasons.

Perhaps the crux of the matter really is simple. If the client wants to storm out of the room the worker will not try to stop him/her physically. However, if the worker feels it necessary to escape from the room because the client is becoming very aggressive and the indications are s/he is about to become violent, then the client obviously would try to stop the worker getting out.

Alarm systems

While workers accept without question or anxiety the presence of fire alarms, notices of what to in the event of fire, and even fire fighting equipment and fire drills, raising the question of installing alarm systems for violent situations seems to cause either considerable anxiety, or disparagement or both in workers. Comments can range from: 'They would only raise unnecessary anxiety and tension in colleagues' to 'We don't need drills because any good worker can talk down any situation so violence won't happen anyway,' and 'When did the last violent situation happen in this office anyway?'

Practical experience of a violent situation, especially when it is a personal experience, tends to remove these objections at a stroke.

Broadly there are two types of alarms, with refinements in each. As both types can be adapted to specific requirements consulting an Alarms systems specialist is advisable. But the firm does need to be made aware of the particular, and in some ways peculiar requirements of the Personal Service Agencies. Though staff security is the purpose of the alarm system, the unusual working relationships Personal Services workers have with their clients requires something different to the more standardised 'strong arm' response pattern to a potential or actual violent situation when they happen in our offices. And that brings in a very different set of criteria to the usual requirements for an alarm system in industrial or commercial premises.

The audible system

This sounds a bell that is heard simultaneously throughout the building in its entirety – and in some versions outside as well. It is like the fire alarm or the alarms in prisons. In prisons the fire alarm and the incident alarm always have a different sound. But it has been known in some Personal Services offices for the incident alarm to be wired into the fire alarm system – so it is the fire alarm that rings when the incident alarm is pressed! No one then knows whether there is a fire indicating everyone should clear the building, or a serious incident when help and back-up is needed for the worker in his/her office. It is likely that the other workers (with any other clients) will rush out of the building leaving the worker under attack alone with his/her assailant.

The benefit of the Audible system (provided it does have a different sound from the fire alarm) is that everyone knows about it and can respond. So, as in a prison, there is a concerted rush to the trouble spot.

But there are, however, several drawbacks:

- The aggressive and angry client will be alerted too, which may cause him/her increased anger or panic, and result in him/her lashing out
- The concerted rush may be 'over-kill' for the particular situation and so aggravate a minor incident, and waste other staff's time as there is no way of telling if it is a serious incident or otherwise
- The preceding drawbacks may make a worker reluctant to use it until there is an extreme situation when it may already have deteriorated too far for it to be retrieved, or for the attack to have actually happened before the back-up has arrived.

The silent system

This sounds a buzzer, only at Reception or some other continually staffed location, and also activates a light on a panel indicating the room where the problem has arisen. The procedure can then involve the office manager or some other designated person who may be any other senior member of staff, who is immediately informed and then goes to the problem area, ideally with another member of staff available to seek additional help if required. The office manager will listen outside the door and then decide on what course of action to take. Alternatives range from:

- Entering the room on a pretext of talking to the worker and then being drawn into the interview by the worker

- Entering the room, making it clear that s/he is there as the office manager to add the element of authority
- Entering to restrain the violent client. Hopefully s/he would have been given the appropriate training
- Entering to restrain, with the other member of staff contacting the police for back-up.

The benefits of the Silent system are:

- The flexibility of response that is possible without the potentially aggressive client being alarmed or aggravated further
- Workers, being aware of that flexibility should be prepared to use the system much earlier in a deteriorating situation rather than delaying until the violence erupts.

The two drawbacks to this system centre around the fact that:

- The response-time is likely to be slightly longer than the 'concerted rush' response because the office manager has to be contacted personally rather than joining in that rush – although people in a rush often get in each other's way.
- If the office manager is out of the habit of ensuring the receptionist knows where s/he is if s/he leaves his/her office to speak to another worker, then valuable time can be lost. So a change in his/her practice might be necessary – but it does easily become a habit.

That delay in response-time should be more than counterbalanced by the alarm being used earlier rather than later and the office manager being told exactly where the trouble-spot is rather than having to hunt for it. In prison, where 'concerted rush' always operates, prison officers have been known to dash right past the room where the problem was actually going and have had to be called back!

Intercoms

There are a variety of intercoms on the market but perhaps the most suitable for the purpose we are considering is the baby alarm intercom. This consists of two units, one of which plugs into the standard 13 amp. wall socket, the other into a similar socket in another room. When switched on everything that is said in the first room is heard in the second. Volume is adjustable. No additional wiring is necessary as the electric ring main of the office building is used.

The set enables a decision to be taken on the type and level of back-up needed and at what speed it is needed. A code word or sentence can be agreed as part of standard office procedure for the worker to initiate back-up being brought in at a lower level of tension before the situation deteriorates towards violence.

This must be a supplement to, rather than a replacement for, an alarm system as it should only be used when some degree of aggression or possible violence is seen as a reasonable possibility. It should not be used for routine interviews. It does require another worker listening at the other end for the whole of the interview and it is likely that this system will rarely be necessary.

As it is not suggested that those interviews should be recorded, this is not illegal, but some might feel it is questionable ethically, even for the more problematic cases.

A client comes to the Personal Services expecting a degree of confidentiality even if they do realise that there are limits set to it. Few Agencies would conceal crime if it is confessed in an interview because there is no legal protection such as that which covers a legal advisor or a priest. And almost all Agencies keep some kind of records, and other Agencies may be brought into the case with the client's knowledge and agreement. Most of these restrictions on the principle of confidentiality are accepted by clients either directly or by implication. But a client would not normally be told about the intercom, so it must only be used with good cause. Of course, a worker may decide for him/herself to tell the client that their conversation is being listened to on that particular occasion – but that interview would then hardly be likely to be productive.

Co-working

The direct alternative to this is to co-work a potentially violent client (see chapter 5) and try to ensure the co-worker is always there when the client comes. But that is highly unlikely to be possible for many reasons (leave, sickness, another call-out, the client arriving unexpectedly) and then the single worker and the office manager will have to decide whether s/he should be seen or not. And what the consequences of that might be.

Co-working is not an answer for the one-off or first-time casual caller and is unlikely to even be possible in a one- or even two-worker office. In the latter much of the time there may be a secretary who could listen on the intercom and who could summon the police if necessary – which may be better than nothing. If they arrive in time.

4 Preventing violence – outside working

When workers are dealing with clients outside the office setting, a different range of safety factors have to be taken into account. The working environment itself is no longer under the worker's control as it is in the office. Consequently safety has to depend far more on the policies and practices that are adopted and practiced, than on any of the physical factors.

There are several situations in which workers will be operating outside the office setting:

Home visits

The major difference between meeting clients in the office and Home visits is that in the latter the worker is on the client's territory, not vice versa. That simple fact alone creates major changes in outlook and basic assumptions, especially as far as the client is concerned.

The concept of 'territory' has very strong connotations and not only for humans. Conflict and strife between animals and even birds as they define and defend their territory for food and habitation are commonplace. And this has continued on into human relationships as the many wars down the centuries testify.

But now in many countries of the modern world 'territory' no longer needs to be defined in terms of areas for hunting or farming which previously were essential for the individual's, the family's and the group's survival, but are now defined more in terms of 'the place where I (or we) live'. That feeling is the same whether it is a country, a town, a mansion, house, flat or even a space on a camping site when a tent is pitched. People who come into the space without 'permission' are regarded as intruders or perhaps invaders. Even when that 'permission' is given, the status accorded to the visitor is very rarely that of 'equal member of the family'. More often it is only that of 'guest', be it with the word 'welcome' in front of it or otherwise.

The status given to workers by clients is perhaps that of 'guest', sometimes 'welcome guest' it is true, but more usually it would be 'visitor' if not 'intruder'. And it is very easy to slip from the status of 'guest' to 'visitor' or even 'intruder'. For a worker to 'act as if they owned the place' is the quickest way to slide to the lowest status as far as the client is concerned.

Workers have to take into account not only the emotional overtones of 'territory', but the legal aspect too. The 'right' of a worker to Home visit without a specific invitation from the client is contained in a Court order which can and does over-ride the normal rights of a householder under Common Law to admit only those s/he wants to. Subject of course, to all those other officials who have the right but which still has to be specifically authorised under Statute.

The authority to visit a client in his/her home is contained in a specific Requirement in a Probation Order (which of course the client has previously agreed to) and in other specific orders such as Parole Licences. But the frequency, duration and degree of intrusion (whether the worker can insist on inspecting the bedrooms for example) is not defined in those Requirements. The frequency is specifically left to the worker's discretion but nothing else is.

Consequently, to a very large degree, the normal rights of a householder still obtains for the client even within those Orders. Without those Orders the worker has no authority contained within the role itself to over-ride any of the normal householder rights at all. In practice many, if not most, workers operate on simply assuming that authority and it not being questioned by the clients who are either somewhat nervous of cross-examining officials or assume that the worker must have that authority or they wouldn't exercise it.

The way in which imposters have presented themselves as Social Workers with the right to physically examine small children and even to take them away from home demonstrates this.

If the client exercises his householder rights and challenges the authority of the worker, if there is no Court Order authorising the worker to do whatever it is s/he is wanting to do, the client may order the worker to leave – and to use 'reasonable force' to eject the worker if s/he does not leave promptly.

The client has the right to decide where the interview will take place, how long it lasts, who sits where, what furniture is where, what weapons are about and whether the dog, ferocious or otherwise, stays in the room. The worker may ask, but it is the client who decides in his/her home.

A police constable has some wider powers but most often s/he still needs Court Orders in the shape of an arrest or search warrant to intrude.

So the worker has to adjust his/her approach to the client, to the contact and, to some extent perhaps, the manner in which the subject matter is dealt with, taking into account this changed power relationship, from worker control to client control.

It is this in particular, which makes executing the right policies, procedures and practices of prime importance.

The worker, in discussion with the office manager in problem cases, has to make that type of decision to take account of all circumstances. It may be decided that there should be no Home visits at all because of a client's history, his/her attitude to the Agency and worker and/or the location of the house. For example, deciding not to visit a male client with a history of sex crimes or violence, living alone in an isolated cottage, especially if a female worker has been assigned the case. On more than one occasion these elementary precautions were not taken with tragic consequences for female workers.

Alternatively, Home visits might be timed to take into account the client's proclivities. There's not much point, and it can prove problematic, to visit an alcoholic in the late afternoon if s/he's likely to have been in the pub at lunchtime. Far better to time the visit between 10.00am and 11.00am when one hopes s/he is reasonably sober.

When one worker did this, and explained to the client why he did it, the client would struggle, and succeed in not reaching for the bottle or beer can until after the worker had left. That was the first step the client took towards controlling his drinking pattern.

The question of back-up, where Home visits to potentially violent clients cannot be avoided, creates particular dilemmas.

It is not at all helpful for a worker to leave a message at the office giving the expected time of return and a suggestion that someone should go to the house if the worker is not back by the specified time. By the time back-up arrives the damage may already have been done to the worker. Alternatively time and resources are wasted if the worker is delayed returning to the office for a multitude of reasons or s/he may have even forgotten to return to the office altogether.

And if the back-up does get to the house and the client says the worker has already left, what can the back-up do that is of any

significance? The worker's battered body might be lying on the
kitchen floor but the back-up cannot demand or force an entry to look.
S/he is not a police constable, nor will s/he have a warrant to do so. S/
he would have to go off to make further enquiries, to check the worker
has not returned subsequently to the office or gone shopping or home.
S/he can only eventually contact the police to see if they can be more
successful in persuading the client to let them in or to get a Magistrates
Warrant if they can't.

Alternatively, the back-up could wait in a car outside the house for
an agreed specific timespan before knocking at the door to check that
everything is alright. But the client has to be asked if s/he is still there
in a casual way rather than as an obvious warning.

This is a better course of action, but still not incident proof.

Another method is for two workers to go together to a potentially
violent Home visit. But this too can provoke a hostile reaction if
normally there is only one worker involved with the case. But that
can be overcome.

Case study

A Worker was telephoned by the wife of an alcoholic. She was very
frightened and begged the worker to go to the house where her husband
had just returned from the pub. He was drunk and was being very
argumentative and threatening. Though it had been stated previously,
quite emphatically to both the alcoholic and his wife that he would not
be interviewed if he was drunk, either at the office (he would get turned
away) nor at the home, the worker took the view that on this occasion
she should give support to the wife by visiting. The worker took her
male office manager with her as back-up whom the client had never
seen before.

When they entered the house the client sneered at the worker, 'So
you've brought your heavy then?' He swung round on the office
manager, 'An' I can lick you dead easy.'

'I'm sure you can,' the office manager said calmly. 'Er – this is your
place, can I sit down please?'

The alcoholic, taken aback at the unchallenging response, and
having it acknowledged that he was 'the boss in his own place' as he
called it, calmed down, told the office manager to sit down, did so
himself and for the rest of the interview talked quite reasonably.

Outdoor group work

There are at least three types of groups that come into this category:
leisure trips such as canoeing or camping, work groups such as tree
planting, fence building for the National Trust among others, and

Community Service projects which are run by the Probation Service. The latter involve people ordered by the courts, as punishment for offences they have committed, to do unpaid work in their leisure time, often at weekends, for the benefit of the wider community.

In all these situations the workers are with clients who are often on those trips or projects precisely because they are violent offenders. They are away from their centres for long periods of time, either hours or days, often in quite remote places. Additionally, on the work groups and Community Service projects the clients are provided with tools that make ideal weapons, e.g. spades, forks, billhooks, axes and hammers.

Community Service projects usually have only one worker with them as the supervisor. Other outside groups are likely to have more, so to some extent they have a degree of built in back-up. But even so, the workers are invariably outnumbered by the clients and from those smaller groups may go off with only one worker.

There are three basic problems that makes any decisions about providing sufficient back-up in numbers and quality to satisfy everyone, almost impossible.

The cost of providing more on-the-spot Workers

Each additional Worker adds to the cost of the project, whatever it is, very rapidly. When every worker has a valid operational role which is readily seen in the routine running of the project by the budget controllers, very little objection to the additional staff can be made. But the suggestion of providing additional workers to be only stand-by back-up would be likely to be opposed as not being cost-effective, until a serious incident does occur. That would then cause second thoughts, and more probably result in the closure of the project altogether rather than providing extra staff. And so save all the money!

The rarity of violent incidents

This is really an aspect of the point above. Can the possibility of violence which can't be quantified, but is not likely to be high, justify the extra costs of the additional staff said to be needed? If the incidents were more frequent and therefore more quantifiable the cost would be justified. But in that event is the project really of sufficient importance to justify putting staff to that degree of risk?

The time factor

When back-up is needed can it quickly reach the incident and so be of any use? When on outside working that factor has three other problems.

- Communication with the centre, which can be readily, if expensively, overcome by the provision of car or mobile telephones or radios.
- What kind and quantity of back-up is to be provided back at the centre on stand-by for callout?
- How long will it take the back-up to actually get to the place where the problem is?

By the time it does arrive is the situation likely to have been resolved anyway?

Not uncommonly the back-up at the Centre consists only of the office or project manager and at times s/he will not be staying at the office for the whole time the project is operating.

It is for all these reasons that it is in this type of work especially, that preventive action is so important. The key is in the careful selection of the two groups of people: the clients and the workers.

The clients

Each client should be selected for the project, not only on the basis of *their* need for the groupwork experience, but also on their capacity to cope with that group's particular pressures and their ability to fit in with the other members of the group.

Should it be considered that there could be problems, especially arising from the latter aspect, the client should be considered for an in-Centre group or another constellation of people in another out-of-Centre group where s/he may fit in better or be more acceptable to the others. In most Community Service situations there is usually a facility to do some in-Centre work.

In no circumstances should a potentially volatile mix of clients be knowingly allowed to congregate simply to make up sufficient numbers for the group to run. The problem should be discussed and, if possible, resolved, but if that mix is not going to work one or more clients should be excluded from the group. It is better to cancel the group altogether than have to be sorrowfully wise after the event.

An example can be when a known child molester is intended to be placed on, say, a Community Service project and threats are made against that client by other members of the group to the Supervisor or Project Manager.

The Workers

Equally important is the selection of workers to run the group. This should not be based on the button-holing of some worker who has the bad luck to be passing at the wrong moment, but a careful selection on the basis of possessing the right skills in the activity being undertaken, knowledge of group dynamics and proven abilities (which could have been assessed while they are working with others on other groups) to run groups either in-Centre or out-of-Centre. The latter is, of course, preferable as that is the kind of situation under consideration. The workers, if more than one, must be in agreement with the objectives of the group and the methods by which those objectives are intended to be achieved. The areas of responsibility must be clearly defined between them so that the workers know them, and so that the clients know that there is a clear structure to the organisation of the group. That makes for confidence in the workers by the clients and less chance for loopholes and contradictions which they can seize on and utilise.

The closing options concept

In out-of-Centre working the 'closing options concept' is more relevant that in almost any other area of work. It is a somewhat grandiose description of a fairly obvious idea. But it is one that is often overlooked or forgotten. It consists of the following figure:

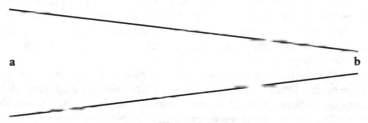

a   b

Figure 4:1

In a situation the variety of options for action closes as time moves on from **a** to **b**. At a the range of options for action may be several or even many. But this range narrows as time passes and the situation deteriorates until only a single option, usually the least desirable, remains.

For example, the worker with a group on a work project or Community Service may see that Joe is very short-tempered this morning. It's possible that he only has a hangover. But he may have had a serious row with his wife that morning, be worried about a sick child or about a forthcoming court appearance the next day. Bill is always clowning around, making comments that he thinks are funny but those on the receiving end often don't.

Options for action at **a** could be for Joe to be talked to to see what the problem is, for Joe and Bill to be kept well apart, for them to be put to work with other people rather than each other, for Bill to be told to cool it, or for Joe to be given a brush to work with rather than a hammer. Or a combination of some or all of the options.

But at **b**, when no action has been taken earlier, the situation explodes and the only options for action left may be to send Joe home (with the other problems that can then arise) and to send for an ambulance for Bill.

Terminating the project or group

Situations can develop in an out-of-Centre group when decisions have to be made by the worker or workers on whether to send individuals home from the project or group, or to close it down altogether, and for all to return to the Centre or go home. It is virtually never a simple decision because of the 'follow-ons' once the decision is taken, whichever one it is.

Sending people home

There are times when the disruption created by an individual client cannot be resolved and finally cannot be tolerated. The disruption to the rest of the group becomes so severe that if that one individual is retained, the rest of the group will suffer too much. So the one, refusing to moderate or alter his/her behaviour, has to be removed from the group.

As those attending groups run by the Personal Services are apt to be the more disruptive rather than the more peaceful and tranquil of people, conflicts between them are liable to arise. Naturally the workers try to get them resolved as soon as possible (see the closing options concept above), finally with clear warnings of being sent home if matters don't change. But the best endeavours may fail and the decision then has to be made. It should be by the general consent of the workers but the Leader has the final responsibility and may have to make the final decision.

If that client is an adult, is capable of travelling by him/herself and there is public transport available, the sending home is comparatively simple. As the organisation has borne the expense of taking him/her to the project, the organisation should ensure the client has the fare to get home by public transport. Hitching can be hit-or-miss and nowadays it is commonsense not to force female clients to try it.

However, a problem can arise if an adult group is in an area with limited or no public transport which can happen if the location is in an isolated or sparsely populated area. This can also be a problem at weekends. A worker from somewhere needs to take that client home from either the project or from the home office area.

Community Service out-of-Centre projects are only likely to have one Supervisor per project, with the home Centre being closed after a short period as the Officer begins to tour some of the projects. If that Officer is not due to visit that particular project the Supervisor is likely to have to close the project altogether for that day. Unless s/he has been provided with a mobile telephone to get the Officer over.

In the case of juvenile clients, the situation is very different. Clearly they cannot travel unaccompanied to their homes, which may be many miles away, by public transport, even if they are given the fares. It is too easy for mishaps to occur and the Leader of the project would still be held responsible for the juvenile client if s/he got into any form of trouble *en route*.

A decision may be made for a worker on the project to take the defaulter home but that may cause difficulties for the project itself because staffing is likely to be tight anyway. An alternative is for the Agency's home office to have the responsibility for collecting a juvenile but those arrangements need to have been made in advance, especially if the project covers a weekend.

Should one Agency be providing a facility to another, it is even more important for those arrangements to have been made beforehand and clearly understood by both Agencies to avoid any misunderstandings. It is very likely that in those circumstances it will be the home Agency that will do any escorting or conveying of defaulting clients.

Terminating the project

This will only be done as a last resort when the problem is one of client misbehaviour. In some ways the problems are fewer as there are none of conveyance or escort – everyone is going. But the mood among the clients is likely to be bad.

There is a different set of problems if there is only one defaulter but only one Supervisor in an area at a time when there is no public transport. The Supervisor (if it is a Community Service project) may decide to close down and take everyone home in his/her car by which the clients were brought to the site. In most Community Service projects the non-defaulters would have the hours credited to them as though they had worked as the fault was not theirs. The defaulter would not have that privilege and could be facing court proceedings for his/her misbehaviour.

The mood of the other clients will vary between delight at getting off early and perhaps disappointment and resentment at the curtailment of an activity they are enjoying and from which they were getting a sense of achievement.

Case study

A worker was suddenly and unexpectedly telephoned by the Chief Executive to travel a distance of over fifty miles to collect two youths from a camp organised by a different Agency but who had been taken from another office of the worker's Agency. The worker had known nothing about this and no arrangement had been made between the Agencies in case this situation should arise. Now it had arisen the home office of the youths were saying they had no worker available to collect the youths. It had been referred to the Chief Executive who telephoned this particular worker, told him to alter his arrangements for the day and, as there were two youths to collect, find another worker to accompany him to go and collect them. By the time the workers arrived at the camp it was mid to late afternoon, the initial telephone call from the camp demanding the removal of the youths having been made first thing that morning.

The workers were greeted only with irritation by the camp officials because of the delay (as they saw it), and then the workers, who did not know the youths themselves, had to go looking for them around the extensive camp area.

They finally arrived at the youths' home area that evening, fortunately finding both sets of parents at home. They were considerably aggrieved as the home office had not even informed them that their sons were being brought home.

Quite obviously, there was scope for disaster at several points as prior arrangements had not been made. It was fortunate that the worker was willing and able to drop his tasks for the day, that he was able to find another worker willing to do the same (in order to comply with the Chief Executive's instruction for there to be two escorting workers) that the youths had stayed on the camp site and that their parents were at home when they finally arrived there.

A problem may arise over the order of dropping off the clients at their homes. The dropping off of the defaulter last can be a recipe for problems even if that would be the usual order. Though clients should not be called upon by the worker to physically assist against other clients, the presence of another person can hold a situation that would otherwise be very difficult.

5   Dealing with the aggressive client

It is in the nature of working with the clients of the Personal Services that measures taken to prevent violence happening will only be able to eliminate a proportion, albeit a large proportion of such incidents. For the clients do have to be interviewed, sometimes when they are in a highly emotional and stressed state of mind. So having reduced the number of aggressive and violent incidents to the lowest possible level by preventive measures, the residue will still need to be coped with.

There are some interviews that can be expected to be stressful by reason of the very nature of, or cause for, the interview. Others will be unexpectedly stressful or confrontational from the first moment, and some will become stressful or confrontational as they progress. The stress may be upon the client, the worker or both, and may result in anger, aggression, violence – or tears.

If a decision has been taken that a child or children must be taken into Care for his/her own safety, then inevitably the interview when the parents are told this will be stressful. Their responses will vary depending on their personalities, Baseline behaviour and the particular circumstances. Many will be fearful, especially if police proceedings are likely. Many will be hostile. Some will be overtly aggressive, threatening to take legal or physical action and some will actually become violent in resisting the action.

A Probation Officer giving a warning to a Parolee or Licencee of a probable recall to prison, if their present behaviour is continued, is in a parallel situation.

A joint meeting with combative parents over Custody of, or Access to, the child/ren in a divorce or matrimonial situation will, of course, double the chances of aggression. It can be between the parents themselves, which may be just a continuation of a previous violent relationship, or upon the worker if s/he should intervene to prevent or stop it, or upon him/her anyway if one parent thinks s/he is supporting the other.

In these foreseeable situations preventive measures involving the choice of interview room, the placing of furniture, ensuring no weapons are available and the seating arrangements, should be taken. But as that interview still has to be conducted the occurrence of a possible explosion is unavoidable.

However, a topic can be introduced by the client without any prior warning which abruptly switches a neutral interview into an emotionally highly charged one.

Indicators

It is very rare that a client, or anyone else, does not give some indication of the way their mood is changing, especially when they are building-up anger.

Body language

As a person's stress levels increase the body tenses for action. This is, of course, the familiar 'fight-flight' syndrome – the body's reaction to a perceived threat or other danger, which will be on the emotional and intellectual level rather than the physical.

Most of these reactions are automatic but some can be consciously controlled. For example, a relaxed body position can be deliberately adopted instead of a tense one. But that kind of compensating action is almost always an exaggerated action and, therefore, usually observable.

An alteration of facial expression or a colouring-up may be the first signs of growing stress and/or anger.

There may be a shifting forward of position to the edge of the chair, a twisting of the body away, or a clenching of the fists.

More obviously, if there is a moving closer to the worker, that 'invasion of personal space' becomes an unspoken threat in itself, especially if the client is taller and bigger than the worker.

That action creates a problem for the worker. If he moves back, if s/he can, the intimidation will be perceived by the client to be working, and then it may be pressed further. If the worker doesn't retreat, the situation becomes more obviously a physical confrontation. To try to push the client away may trigger an assault – and, in any case, is a technical assault. If the worker stands up from a sitting position, which is itself vulnerable, that may be seen as a response threat by the client. S/he may back off, but s/he may not. A worker who stood up to intervene between a husband who had suddenly got up to tower threateningly over his wife, was grabbed by the throat by the husband.

There are no easy answers!

Threatening gestures, especially a fist held against the worker's face, clearly indicates a certain frame of mind!

Looks

A client's way of looking at the worker or at another client may alter. A glare commonly indicates anger. A stare may indicate something else.

> **Case study**
> A worker interviewing a paranoid client and his wife noticed that the client had begun to tensely watch the worker's hands. The worker, who until that moment had been making his usual style of small hand gestures while talking, began to make fewer gestures and then folded his hands and made no more. He did not comment on the client's stare nor asked the reason for it. But the client began to relax and eased his fixed stare on the worker's hands. Later the worker discovered that it had suddenly occurred to the client that the hand gestures were really a sign language to the wife, telling her what to say.

A rapid eye search around the room for potential weapons, obstacles between client and worker or other intended victim, or for the best spot to land a punch may be noticed.

Voice

As anger mounts, the voice alters. Usually it becomes louder as the angry person shouts, but a few people begin to speak more quietly but with more intense feeling. The voice may become shaky, deeper, more shrill or stiff-lipped. It is the fact that the voice has altered that is significant, not necessarily the form that alteration takes.

Language

As a person becomes angry, language or the choice of words becomes more aggressive. There is a greater tendency to swear (to give added emphasis by the stronger adjectives) to de-personalise the worker by using racist, sexist, or demeaning descriptions, and to move on to direct threats.

Some workers take the view that a client shouting and threatening indiscriminately is 'ventilating his/her feelings' and this should not be stopped or even discouraged in any way, even when others are frightened by it.

However, if that type of behaviour is sanctioned by the worker (even if only by implication) at what point can that client's self-control be encouraged and developed? To say to the client s/he should be more self-controlled when s/he is calm anyway, is irrelevant. It is obviously very relevant when s/he is throwing a tantrum, when a command to, 'Sit down and be quiet' given in a firm, emphatic tone, can be surprisingly effective.

Counselling techniques

As the tension and stress begins to build in an interview the worker should have a range of techniques to hand to use to maintain or regain control of the interview.

Workers will have been trained in these techniques and be using them in his/her day-to-day work when calming distressed clients, reducing tensions between clients and interceding between clients and other Agencies. These same techniques still apply as tense situations deteriorate towards aggression and violence. They can still be used after an assault actually happens.

Person-to-person contact

From the outset of any interview it is a basic principle that it is normally better to establish contact at a person-to-person level rather than the worker to take a 'superior public official' stance. A client who is already feeling aggressive against an Agency is not likely to react favourably to heavy-handed officialese.

An exception to this general principle is when the office manager has to come into a situation as 'back-up'. Then, an authoritative approach is usually the right one.

The 'we' approach

Another basic principle to be maintained as things begin to deteriorate, is the 'sharing' approach to problem solving. This can be disarming to the client because he/she won't want to turn a friendly, possibly helpful and even powerful ally, into another antagonist.

This approach may not be possible if it is a 'crunch' interview (e.g. warning of a possible recall to prison if the client keeps on with his/her unacceptable behaviour) until things progress towards an understanding of, and dealing with, the factors lying behind that unacceptable behaviour.

Case study
One office manager deliberately adopted that authoritative stance, explaining he was the Senior Probation Officer and stating he was ordering the drunken youth out of the Waiting Area where he was being noisy and troublesome. The youth's excuse for being there was that he was waiting for a friend who was being seen by one of the Probation Officers.

But on another occasion that same office manager intervening in a fraught situation geared his approach to the fact that he had had some slight acquaintance with the aggressive client over ten years before. He adopted the 'cheerfully smiling, friendly, personal' approach, totally ignoring the tense atmosphere between the client and the worker. He reminded the client who he was (the client obviously didn't remember him at all) shook his hand, asked how he was getting on, how his mother was and what was he doing now.

Totally taken aback the client nevertheless responded to this approach, the atmosphere was calmed and the problems eventually resolved.

De-personalising the issue

This is different from de-personalising a person. For example, the question of a worker giving money to a client (when that is not the primary function of the Agency) is fraught with problems. The client often assumes that the process of giving him/her some money is wholly and totally under the control of their particular worker, which nowadays is rarely the case. If the worker is under the constraints of office or Agency controls and cash limits, explaining that that is the case and why, can often remove the 'blame' that the disgruntled client is putting on the worker. It also helps the client to face the reality of the situation that both they and the worker are in. Any effort then made by the worker to resolve the problem some other way is likely to be seen positively by the client.

Obviously promises that cannot be met made simply to calm a difficult immediate situation must not be made, tempting though it may be. Any calming effect at that stage will only rebound in greater resentment by the client when the worker is found out, possibly at the very next interview. Mistrust in workers generally, and this one in particular, will deepen.

If the workers promises to *attempt* something, that is a different matter. But it must then be emphasised to the client that it is a promise to *try* – but there can be no promise or guarantee of success. Because of a natural tendency to hear what is wanted to be heard not necessarily what is actually said, that point will need a lot of repeated emphasis.

Listening

Listening should be carried out on three levels.

Listening to the words that are being said
The worker must fully engage in the discussion that is taking place, and be seen by the client to be doing so. This is a basic casework precept which reduces the likelihood of an aggressive reaction and is also courteous. Not being visibly fully engaged in the discussion will be interpreted by the client as indifference to his/her problems. And that is the last thing a client in a crisis can take. By using particular words the client is trying to get across exactly what his/her needs are, and how urgent they are.

Perceiving the emotions behind the words
These are conveyed by the voice and tone, the posture and demeanour of the facial expressions and the movements of the eyes. By being alert to these, the worker's responses will be appropriate, helpful and calming.

Planning responses if the client's aggression rises and the possibility of violence increases
A useful response is that of humour, not directed *at* the client, nor ridiculing him/her, but to laugh *with* the client at something exterior to them both. Some people seem to have a natural talent for this, and produce a positive response, others don't.

A worker can, by offering a cigarette or cup of coffee, removing the trigger, moving his/her position or even changing of the interviewing room altogether, introduce a physical change which can help change the mood.

An experiment with a group of workers demonstrated that men in a confrontational situation when both are standing, tend to stand face-to-face and toe-to-toe. When talking in a relaxed way they tend to stand at a slight angle to each other. Women in similar situations are much less clear-cut in their body stances.

So if there is a confrontational situation when both men are standing, if one turns slightly away from the other while continuing to talk, tension will be reduced. If the other turns to make it into a face-to-face confrontation again, another move a little while later (so you don't get into a spinning system!) will produce the same effect.

Workers who have had cause to use this technique have assured me it does work. Another advantage is that it makes the worker less of a full-frontal target if physical violence happens.

As a nearly-last resort, when the client seems on the verge of losing self-control and moving forward dangerously, a sharp, 'Stop that!' can sometimes be effective when given with confidence and authority. If the order is given in anxiety or panic the wrong tone of voice will be used and will convey an impression of weakness and indecision which will, of course, make it less effective.

The climax of the incident

At this point all the preventive measures of the Agency and the casework skills of the worker have failed to control the situation and violence is about to erupt. The timespan from the beginning of tension to its climax may be long or a matter of a few seconds. The violence of the client may be directed against another client or the worker.

The worker should never precipitate violence by any physical contact (e.g. pushing the client away) if that can possibly be avoided. Case law, though not Statute law, indicates that physical retreat as far as may be reasonable and practicable should be made.

Getting between clients to prevent one assaulting the other has worked successfully for me three times, on the fourth occasion it led to the attack being switched to me.

When the violence does happen it can be as short as a single blow or it may be a longer sustained attack.

If it is a single blow, the worker must not retaliate because legally the attack would then be over. So a follow-up by the worker is not seen as self-defence but in legal fact turns the worker, who had been the victim, into the aggressor. And the original aggressor into the victim.

If the attack is sustained, other measures become necessary. Leave the room if that is possible and does not leave other vulnerable people, such as children, alone with the violent aggressor. Summon back-up if that is not already there. Use restraint if the attack is pressed and training has been received. If the violent client has been locked in a restraint hold, it is as well to be cautious about fully accepting the first declaration of passivity and good intentions. It has happened that people have 'played passive' and made promises of good behaviour until released – and then started again.

In the final analysis a restraint hold by the worker may not be possible because of the degree of violence used and/or the style of the attack, differences in size and build, an age or physical handicap factor or lack of expertise or knowledge of the techniques by the worker.

Then the decision has to be made about Self-Defence action, or submission to a beating or worse. The Self-Defence may consist of a flailing about in sheer panic, or action under more rational control.

To be effective in a situation that requires Restraint or Self-Defence, training in these techniques is necessary, because panic reactions are not likely to be good enough.

The emotions of rage and the physical violence are exhausting for the aggressor as well as the recipient, especially as the adrenalin begins to ebb. So high levels of aggression will last only for a certain period before the aggression itself begins to lag through sheer tiredness. That though, can take a considerable time and a lot of damage can be done before it finally happens.

After the incident

Action in the immediate aftermath will clearly depend on the seriousness of the attack. The police may have been called and the aggressor arrested. Medical treatment may be necessary, either First Aid or hospital treatment.

If the violence has been minimal, with little or no injury, it may be possible to simply sit down and start working again at the problem with the client.

Other administrative action will be necessary as in the medium and longer term, after all violent incidents, other decisions will need to be made and actions taken.

6 The race factor in violence

'All human beings are born free and equal in dignity and rights. They are endowed with reason and conscience and should act towards each other in a spirit of brotherhood.'

'Everyone is entitled to all the rights and freedoms set forth in this Declaration, without distinction of any kind, such as race, colour, sex, language, religion, political or other opinion, national or social origin, property, birth or other status.' Articles 1 and 2, Universal Declaration of Human Rights.

The definition of the word 'race' has changed over time but the Race Relations Act 1976 has now set the definition – 'racial group' means 'a group of persons defined by reference to colour, race, nationality, or ethnic or national origins and references to a person's racial group refer to any racial group into which he falls.' Sec. 3(1).

As British society struggles to come to terms with being a multiracial and multi-cultural society, racial attitudes and racism are contributory factors to the overall level of violence in British society.

Racist behaviour, as well as urban deprivation, was identified as a major contributing cause to the riots in British cities during the 1980s. In order to defend themselves against racist attacks and harassment some communities have decided to form watch-groups as they believe the police force has been persistently inactive in responding to complaints about such attacks.

But racial attitudes and racism are not unique to Britain and to the present day. Knowing that does not, however, reduce in any way the wrongs that are committed here and now. Racial persecution, and what is now being called 'ethnic cleansing,' has caused misery across the world for thousands of years. It has been inflicted by, and on, many different peoples and groups as testified in both written histories and stories passed down through the generations by word-of-mouth.

To discount the experience of all those people, arguing that it is not relevant to the experience of black people in Britain today, is to lose sight of the lesson that this history teaches – the principle which, when taken to the extreme, results in racial attitudes and thence racism: that every in-group (those who identify with each other) has out-groups (all those that that particular in-group excludes from itself). The raison d'etre for in-groups is the support for each other in the existence of shared interests, shared politics, shared work, shared misfortune, shared rejection, shared religion, shared nationality or shared skin colour. Each in-group reacts to its out-groups somewhere along a continuum of tolerance-to-intolerance. Where that point lies on the continuum will depend on the reasons for that in-group existing, the history of the cultures around that in-group, the degree of 'threat' that the in-group is seen as posing by the out-group, myths about the in-group and finally individual's own prejudices.

Every group that is an in-group to itself is an out-group to someone else. As an example, in the 1930s the Jews in Germany were an in-group to themselves, and the Nazi Party an out-group. The converse was also true – the Nazis saw themselves as an in-group and the Jews as an out-group. As the Nazis gained power, first locally and later nationally, they used that power immediately and devastatingly on their out-group, the Jews.

It is that same principle of in-groups and out-groups that operates in Britain today. History, myths, and prejudices of individuals influence the out-working of that principle. Britain's colonial history, myths around it, and the effects of that on the predominant white culture and socially transmitted norms, produce racial attitudes. Though it is reasonably valid to speak of a 'predominant white culture', that culture is not homogeneous – there are wide differences within it influenced by social, geographical and educational (e.g. race awareness courses) factors.

Racial attitudes and racism

There is a significant and fundamental difference between racial attitudes and racism which turns on who possesses and can exercise coercive power.

Racial attitudes

This is when an individual of any race regards others of another race with disfavour or disdain, with the corollary that they regard themselves as superior to those others.

This means that racial attitudes based on the in-group, out-group principle, are multi-directional; they are not restricted to only one race directing them against one other race.

Case studies

Examples of this attitude include white people's attitudes towards black people which range from persecution and abuse of power to a passing comment by a woman who regarded herself as non-racist, 'He's black but he's very nice though', as if the two facts together were surprising. She then realised what she had said and became embarrassed.

A black client went to see his worker taking his small child with him. A secretary who was white asked him if he would like her to look after the child whilst he was with his worker. The client immediately refused. Later, the secretary asked the worker why the client had refused and was told that the client considered 'they were white trash' and unsuitable to look after his child.

There are many examples of black against black and white against white racial attitudes: from ethnic conflicts in Africa (Idi Amin expelling many Asians from Uganda), Germans against European Jews in the Holocaust, ethnic conflicts in the former Soviet Union and Yugoslavia as they have broken up.

Racism

This is when racial attitudes are demonstrated and enforced by coercive power. But there are different kinds and levels of 'power'. There are the lawmakers in Parliament and Local Authorities with grant-giving powers, there are commanders who give orders to troops, there are people acting as a group under their own control and at their own initiative, and ultimately there is an individual acting against another individual in an immediate and local situation.

A white landlord refused to let a flat to a black enquirer. Clearly, it is the landlord who has the power in that situation.

A black employer refused a job to a white applicant. Clearly, it is the employer who has the power in that situation.

A white policeman, motivated by racial attitudes, harasses a black youth. He is in a position of power, so that becomes a racist act.

A black policeman, motivated by racial attitudes, harasses a white youth. He is in a position of power, so that becomes a racist act.

A worker refuses a request from a client. It is s/he who has the power in that situation by reason of their respective roles, whatever the race of the two may be.

The conclusion is that racial attitudes can be shown by anyone against anyone. Racism is when those racial attitudes are shown in a power situation that is local in space and time. It is personal but it can also be institutionalised which then is seen as sanctioning covert or overt racism by individuals, even though the written laws condemn it, as in Britain today.

The feeling of powerlessness

Very many black people from all walks of life in Britain today speak of having a feeling of powerlessness in a white-dominated society. They draw upon their own experience and that of others as the reason for this.

When people consider they are members of a group that is discriminated against, every example of such discrimination against an individual reinforces that belief as it is told to others. Examples of non-discrimination are usually lost sight of in that overall feeling of the individual. So the belief, founded on fact and reinforced by experiences, even when countered by other experiences, is not contradicted and so grows and deepens. This then influences perceptions of, and responses to, contacts, just as a victim of violent crime thereafter has a heightened awareness of what constitutes 'threat', and may see that where none is intended.

That feeling of powerlessness to change things, coupled with the feeling of rejection by the wider society that those people live in, can produce alienation from that society. That alienation may result in a person deciding to withdraw and to stay within their own in-group to a greater or lesser degree, at times holding determinedly onto all their traditional attitudes, values and behaviour. Others will move partly into that wider society. Others will move into that society on what they see as that society's terms. Others will decide to fight that society.

The decision to fight, when made by individuals, may result in a pattern of life of breaking the laws of that society in various ways. When those individuals form groups that are small they may simply continue the lawbreaking on an individual basis. Some form political groups and may coalesce to become a major political force.

Racial attitudes and behaviour – the worker in the personal services

To influence people sufficiently to cause them to change attitudes in general is difficult, and racial attitudes are perhaps the most difficult of all to change. There are two factors that make this difficulty:

1. Racial attitudes have their origins in the past history which has influenced, and still influences, the cultural traditions and therefore the socially transmitted norms of the white British culture.
2. The difficulty white people have of fully understanding what it is like to be a black person in a predominantly white culture in which there is generally an underlying assumption of white superiority, with a great deal of overt racist behaviour being shown by some and unrealised and often unintended racial comments made by many.

These experiences, which perhaps every client has experienced to a greater or lesser degree will inevitably affect his/her own attitudes, perceptions and expectations of any new contact with another worker especially if white, in another Agency.

Consequently changing racial attitudes will be long-term rather than short-term and will take pressures from many directions: legal, cultural and social.

Those in the Personal Services in particular have a special role in this, working as they do at the interface between their clients (who are often the most discriminated against) and other parts of society which may have considerable power as far as their clients are concerned, and other people who may have and show racial and racist attitudes and behaviour.

So workers themselves have a need to understand as far as possible, the reality of a black client's experience and situation and to accept that client's culture is as 'valid' as his/her own, and that the basic ethos and value of the Personal Services – the worth of the individual applies to all equally. This means that workers in the Personal Services must be anti-racist.

Though all Personal Service Agencies must view this seriously it cannot be assumed that each and every worker necessarily has the same awareness of, and sensitivity to, these issues. Workers are inevitably in a position of power *vis-à-vis* their clients, which equally inevitably means those clients are vulnerable if racial discrimination is practiced either overtly or covertly. So specific awareness training on these issues is necessary for workers of all grades.

Though *attitudes* are difficult to change, *behaviour* can be changed more quickly, given the right pressures. Behaviour is relatively easy to monitor and so challenge, whereas an attitude can be concealed.

It is therefore necessary for an Agency to have a very clearly defined and carefully explained policy of non-discriminatory practices for workers to adhere to. This needs to be backed-up by the monitoring of those standards to ensure, as far as is possible, that they are being complied with, and with appropriate action being taken when they are not.

The Practice Instructions will need to be wide-ranging and cover *inter alia*:

- The advertising of posts
- Selection for those posts
- Training – specifically in the Agencies Policy and Practice Instructions and the Race Relations Act 1976 and as appropriate on other courses
- A defined anti-discrimination policy
- The establishing of links with ethnic communities
- Monitoring – of all aspects of work as a specific factor at intervals and as an element in other monitoring
- A clearly defined and effective Complaints Procedure which is made known to the Agency's clients.

The effects of discrimination

On the client

When clients are discriminated against on racial grounds, they are faced with a problem, the basis of which they cannot change by any effort they may make – for a person's racial origins are fixed. Everyone's is. Inevitably. As that cannot be changed a victim's only solution is for change in the discriminating practices that are being exercised by others.

If a service, legitimately asked for, is refused on racial grounds, the frustration that anyone feels at the refusal of a request is engendered, as well as a deeper and hurting sense of grievance for being treated in such a way for something over which the client has no control and cannot change. A sense of inferiority, if already there, is reinforced by a sense of helplessness and powerlessness at being unable to alter the situation. Resentment and anger will be induced and the client's attitude towards the worker personally, and their Agency in general, will be poisoned.

And it is inevitable, that if the client is refused benefits to which s/he is entitled, whether on racial grounds or others, the standard of life for him/her and his/her family is lowered still further.

On the Worker

There may be one of two repercussions:

The use of the Complaints Procedure

The Agency, as part of its overall responsibility, needs to have a clearly defined Complaints Procedure. But also the client needs to know about it and how to call upon it.

Some clients, especially in settings such as prisons, feel and in many ways are, so powerless against those people with the power in that system (i.e. all staff) that they are convinced that their next case would be worse than their last if they were to make a complaint against one of them. And so they are often unwilling to make a complaint even when they feel one is justified.

But such a complaint against a worker is so serious a matter, in any setting, with such serious consequences, that it is only natural justice that the accused worker should be able to face his/her accuser and for cross-examination of both sides to be possible. So the client's presence is essential to any Enquiry or Disciplinary Hearing.

The client can therefore be in a double-bind situation: if no complaint is made the discriminator has got away with it and is likely to continue his/her behaviour against both that individual and others, but if s/he does complain there may be worse problems if the discriminator stays in his/her position or his/her colleagues decide to act against the client in support of the discriminator.

So the Complaints Procedure must have a protection element for the client as an essential part of it. The simplest way is to remove the alleged discriminator from that client to work elsewhere. Or, in a serious situation, from all clients by suspension.

A complaint against a worker may be made to his/her Agency's Management and be dealt with internally by means of an Enquiry or Disciplinary Hearing, or it may be referred to the Council for Racial Equality or it may be taken to the County Court by a Civil Action under the Race Relations Act 1976. If the Worker's alleged behaviour falls within the Race Relations Act Sec. 69 (making false or misleading statements) or the Public Order Act 1986 Sec. 17 (inciting racial hatred) then the police will need to be involved, as those are criminal offences.

Violence or aggression

If there is no Complaints Procedure, or if the client believes it to be ineffective, or if there is no built-in protection element for the client, in desperation or frustration the client may lash out in verbal aggression or physical violence against a worker, perhaps as being the latest discriminator but in any case a the handiest representative of a discriminating and oppressive society. The force of the client's reaction to the immediate situation may be out of all proportion to it, but this discrimination may have been just the latest of a series of bad experiences.

On the Agency

No Personal Services Agency in Britain can have a policy of racial discrimination.

However, the workers of any Agency (or indeed any kind of employer) can operate a system to sabotage an Agency (or any employer) policy. Despite all the monitoring of anti-racism standards that can be devised, in practice an Agency's policies can only be as good and effective as the workers make them. If, in their one-to-one contacts with clients, workers practice discrimination (which of course they will not record) an Agency will not even be aware of it until there is a complaint.

But the standing of that Agency would have already been damaged among its clients and their resentment against and mistrust of, the wider society will have been increased. Should the matter come to the notice of the media, either local or national, the resultant publicity will be immensely damaging.

The black worker, white client situation

Just as racial attitudes can affect the relationships between white workers and black clients, so they can affect them between black workers and white clients.

Localities

Racial attitudes vary in strength in different localities, even between different areas of the same town. In very general terms, some areas do not show strong racial attitudes against minorities living in them, whether the minorities are black people living in predominantly white areas, white people living in predominantly black areas or in highly mixed areas. Those individuals who might hold racial attitudes as 'principles' in those areas will tend to say that the people they know are 'different' from the racial stereotypes they hold – without being able to say exactly what those 'differences' are!

But there are other areas (more likely to be white) where racial and racist attitudes are strong, verbalised and acted out. In these areas a black worker visiting a client's home may run into harassment of a greater or lesser degree from bystanders, because s/he is a black person rather than being a black worker. Unless s/he is known as a worker – and usually they don't like workers either!

This situation may create a genuine problem for the client. S/he may or may not have racial attitudes him/herself but would be expected to have them by his/her friends and neighbours and to be antagonistic to, and unco-operative with, the black worker. The client is then caught between peer group pressure and the lack-of-power s/he is in in relation to the worker.

In that situation, if the client requests it, should the worker be changed? Or is that to be considered a bowing to a racial attitude by the client whatever the reason for the request? Or is it to be seen as pressure from his/her neighbours which must still be rejected irrespective of how the degree of co-operation from the client may be affected by the conflict s/he is in? For that conflict is likely to develop into resistance, aggression or possible violence as the pressure from the two sides builds-up on the client.

The power relationship

As 'power' is shown and experienced in an immediate situation it is a highly relevant factor when client and worker meet face-to-face. Apart from the caveats of Territory (see chapter 1) it is usually the worker who is in the power position. Commonly, it is that factor which makes a client decide to keep any racial attitudes s/he may have under wraps, even when they are fairly strong. This is particularly so in the custodial situation.

Whether the worker is based in an institution or visiting a client there, commonly the client will believe that to show racial attitudes against the worker is likely to have adverse conse- quences for him/herself either immediately (e.g. a request being refused by the worker) or in the future (by an adverse report).

But that is only 'commonly', not 'always'. Some clients will not care anyway. Abusive catcalls may come from the anonymity of a crowd. Other clients may erupt if a request is refused, their temper flares and they decide they have nothing to lose by showing their real attitudes.

The professional relationship

Very occasionally an apparently racial attitude verbalised by a client is thought by them to cause fewer problems than being frank about his/ her other reasons, and so uses it as a convenient 'get out'. Which demonstrates how deep racial attitudes are with some having little or no conceptions of the implications of what they are saying.

Case study
A black worker described, when preparing a report for the Court on a young white offender on a Criminal Damage charge, that when he interviewed the youth three times and met his parents he found no problems over racial attitudes from any of them at all. The boy was put on supervision to that worker which was fully acceptable to him and his parents. During the preparation of the report, when this recommendation was discussed with them, the worker had made clear what his expectations would be of the client. During the order the worker enforced them. Within a short time the boy asked for a change of worker. After some questioning he said it was 'because the worker was a black man'. This was discussed at some length in the worker's Team Meeting and the decision made that in all the circumstances there was no need for the worker to be changed. The boy accepted the decision without argument and co-operated fully. Towards the end of the order the subject was raised again. This time the boy said that it had not really been because the worker was black that he asked for the change, but because the worker was strict and the client thought he would get an easier ride from someone else. But he could hardly say that. The worker believed that this had been the boy's real reason.

Throughout contact with the client the worker must maintain his/ her professional stance even when the client is trying to bring the relationship down to a personally racially abusive level.

The worker will have an understanding of the cultural background of the client's racial attitudes and the reasons for his/her current reactions to the immediate situation. Also the worker will have the personal maturity to be able to cope with this behaviour even though it is felt to be personally insulting, and/or irritating, and/or hurtful.

The black worker, black client situation

The antithesis to the earlier situation is when a black client seeks to utilise the shared 'blackness' of the worker and him/herself by making it a bond from which the client tries to pull special privileges or advantages.

Because there will be a level of genuine 'sharing' there is a danger that the worker's objectivity may vary from its usual professional standard.

But when that client finds s/he is not accorded any special and privileged treatment s/he may turn from that 'companionship' attitude to one of rejection, antagonism or even violence.

Black clients, culture and violence

It is an element in the racial attitudes of many white people that there is a belief that black people are more violent than white people. So white people may avoid black people whenever possible, especially groups of black youths.

There seem to be two factors that influence this assumption: a belief that if there is a difference in skin colour there must be a difference in culture, and therefore in behaviour and proneness to violence; and secondly a lumping together of all the many individuals into one stereotype.

Are different cultures more violent?

Cultures do vary from country to country and, as those cultures meet, there is invariable a degree of culture clash followed, over lengthy periods lasting for generations, by a large degree of merging until a new culture emerges. When there is conquest and the invaders impose their culture the merging is somewhat quicker than when there are peaceful movements of populations.

In Britain at the present time the merging with the more recent population inflows has barely begun, though it is happening. The Notting Hill Carnival is an example of elements of the Caribbean being brought to England and expanding the long established British custom of processions and local displays such as the Marching Bands and Morris Dancers.

Wherever and whenever cultures have met there has always been a measure of culture clash because the customs, practices and values of the two have differed. Initially they seem strange to each other, then some, usually among the younger generations, finds the other culture is interesting and provides new experiences and they adopt some parts, initially perhaps some practices and customs but then some of their values. This can then cause arguments between the generations within family units as the younger generations challenge the established behaviour patterns and eventually the values of the older members of their respective cultures.

A study of the incoming cultures of recent years shows there is no basis for the belief that they have brought with them the belief that violence should be part of normal everyday life, and that therefore its members will automatically be more violent in their ordinary dealings with other people. It is individuals within all cultures, including the white British culture, that choose to be violent for many and varied reasons.

Different people, same stereotype?

The question itself assumes that most or all people in the black population, with all their varied ethnic backgrounds coming from many different parts of the world with widely varying cultures, all fit into the same stereotype – that all will show more violent behaviour more readily than those people in the white population.

Personal contact quickly shows that people in the black section of the community are as varied in personality, attitudes, outlooks and personal values as all other racial groups; that all are individuals and cannot be forced into a single stereotype.

7 The gender factor in violence

'All workers and clients are either male or female.' This statement is obvious, but introduces additional complexities to the already complicated skein of factors involved in violent relationships.

In very general terms, many men in Britain share some assumptions and attitudes about women, just as women do about men. Because Britain is a multi-cultural society, each of those cultures is made-up of sub-cultures, each of which, in turn, have their own shades of those widely shared assumptions and attitudes. Those sub-cultures in turn are made up of family and even individual shades of that sub-culture's view.

Sometimes those differences can cause surprises.

Case study
A newly trained worker, from Kent, arrived in a foundry and steelmaking town on the edge of the West Midlands nearly thirty years ago. In his first months a casual caller arrived at the office to talk about the changes in behaviour of her husband. She explained he was a foundry worker who regularly got drunk at weekends when he would occasionally beat her.

With total seriousness she went on, 'But now he's taken to getting drunk on a Wednesday as well and comes home and knocks me about more. Well, you expect that a man who works hard all week'll get drunk at the weekends and then knock you about a bit. That's normal. But it's a bit much when he does it in the week too."

That was a new view of things to that worker as he hailed from a community where that particular outlook would not be the norm.

In the Personal Services, especially perhaps the Probation Service about thirty years ago, the tendency was that male workers dealt with male clients and female workers dealt with female and child clients. But inevitably there was overlap because male clients had female partners and female clients had male partners resulting in some cross-gender work.

Then views changed and the norm became that any worker would deal with any client, except in exceptional cases when, for special reasons, a same-gender worker would be specifically selected.

But now there is a swing back towards same-gender working as increasing evidence shows the effects of child sexual abuse can extend into adulthood, and that those effects can most suitably be dealt with using same-gender workers. It is claimed that all female clients, in particular, should have female workers in case their problems were caused or influenced by child sexual abuse.

How far that view will extend remains to be seen.

But these changes do reflect the many other changes in assumptions and attitudes that have taken place over time though some do seem to have changed little for many in the population.

The workers' perspective

The male Worker

For workers, as for clients, assumptions and attitudes are the product of their past and present environments as modified by any thinking and decisions they may have made as individuals. That combination of influences accounts for the individual's shadings of views within a generalised norm.

The outcome of that process, which still continues, will inevitably influence the worker's approach to his/her work but especially to cross-gender work. The worker mentioned earlier, having the assumptions that all and any violence to women was morally wrong, and totally inexcusable as well as illegal, was considerably taken aback at the client's acceptance of it – provided it was limited to weekends only. He was even more taken aback when she decided she wanted nothing done to change the situation. She felt she was better off than many of her neighbours who got beaten more often than she was, and were kept short of money as well, something from which she didn't suffer.

In such a case a male worker may feel that he should take on the role of becoming the 'protector' of the female client against the abusing husband, especially when the behaviour was so contrary to his own values and assumptions. But was that approach appropriate when that client, who had her own set of assumptions, accepted that behaviour as part of her norm and insisted on no action being taken? Can workers project their *own* assumptions, attitudes and values upon their clients? And then pressure the clients to accept them? Are there objective standards of behaviour, assumptions and attitudes that are the 'right' ones? And can workers in the Personal Services presume that they hold the 'right' attitudes to matters other than those prescribed in law?

The female Worker

Case study
A client went to a Clinic for a routine check-up and was asked by her clinic worker about her relationship with her husband whom the worker had never met. The client said 'They were going through a bad patch', her husband bullied her and sometimes hit her. The worker said she wouldn't tolerate *her* husband hitting her and nor should the client. Why didn't she leave him?

There was more discussion and eventually the client said she did want to leave her husband but where could she go? The worker immediately contacted another Agency to ask them to arrange for the client to go to a Women's Refuge. When the worker from the other Agency discussed it with the client she recognised some reluctance on the part of the client although she said she still wanted to leave. After one night's stay in the Refuge the client went to her mother's home.

That day her husband went to confront the worker of the Agency, not the Clinic. A violent incident took place at the office and her parent's home that lasted for several hours, resulted in an Agency Worker being assaulted and the police being called to the house to arrest the husband.

Later that evening the client went of her own initiative to the police station where her husband was in custody to say she had decided to return to him and had never really wanted to leave him at all.

It had not been possible to ascertain whether the client was really wanting help to solve the problem of where to go, or was just trying the refuge as a way out of what she saw as a pressurised situation. As she was able to go to her mother's home it seems that the latter was the reason.

Clearly the Clinic worker brought her own assumptions into the situation and allowed her own emotions to affect her advice. Perhaps the Agency worker was more sensitive to and perceptive of, the client's views, not allowing her own views of violent husbands (which were strong) to influence her work, though necessarily she acted on the statements made.

Working with a rapist

Although virtually all workers will experience fear in one situation or another, many or perhaps most, female workers will be likely to feel vulnerable sexually and/or physically when faced with a client who is known to be a rapist, particularly if the violence element in the rape(s) was towards the heavy end of the violence continuum.

For that reason, and because there can be the very real possibility of the offence or some element of the offence (i.e. the violence or sexual element) of the offence being repeated, it is both sensible and appropriate for such cases to be handled either by a male worker or by cross-gender co-working. In the latter event, decisions will need to be made in advance about the action to be taken if only the female worker is in the office when that client calls or telephones in asking for an urgent Home visit.

The clients' perspective

The male client

It is rare for male clients to have previously thought deeply about or reached any understanding of the deeper aspects of the nature of the relationships between the genders. Although they may have heard of the concept of 'Sexual Equality' and 'Equal Opportunities' as a result of an isolated case hitting the media headlines, few would have concluded it had anything to do with them and their everyday contact with females, especially if their environments had been and were currently ones where the male was dominant.

When it comes to the type of relationship to have with a female worker of an Agency, especially a Statutory Agency in which the role carries with it certain coercive powers (e.g. Breach of Probation or Parole), there may be a conflict between the client's expectation of being able to dominate 'just another female' (even if she does happen to be a worker) and a degree of reluctance to try that, just in case the worker does 'turn nasty' (from the client's point of view) and suddenly uses the sanctions against him.

The dilemma for him is not eased if the female worker insists on being called by her first name in the interests 'of building a good relationship'. That can indicate to a client unused to the ways of Personal Service Workers, that really the worker wants to be treated on a personal relationship basis rather than an 'official' (professional) one. In that case, until he learns differently by hard experience, he is likely to assume he can dominate her by pressure or blandishment if that is the nature of his other personal relationships with females.

Attempts to dominate the worker by pressure is far more obvious and easily recognised and so resisted, but it may be more difficult for a worker (of either gender) to resist the moves of 'seduction' from a client of the opposite gender if s/he is friendly, responsive and personable. After all, those are the bases of the development of ordinary relationships.

However, the relationship of a worker and client is not 'normal' in that sense, it is a professional one. But some clients see it as a useful policy to try to move it to a friendship (at least) relationship. As males, currently, are usually the initiators of such moves, they may well try that tactic, especially conmen to whom this is their stock-in-trade.

If this happens problems will arise when the worker realises what is going on and then, apparently inconsistently to the client, begins exercising authority.

Bewildered, the client may then withdraw, deciding that all women are unpredictable and that he won't trust *that* worker again. Or he may try to enforce his believed domination by becoming aggressive or violent especially as his macho-man self-image has been damaged.

Other male clients will approach a female worker from a different starting point, especially if the worker is a more mature woman. They will adopt a virtual dependant child-to-mother role, seeking constant support, material help, advice and sympathy. And when any or all are not forthcoming in copious quantities, will either sulk or throw a childlike tantrum, which, because they are not children in size and strength, may well be alarming. Also, just as an uncontrolled child can become violent against the frustrator, so can the uncontrolled adult.

The male client's approach to a male worker will be based on different assumptions and attitudes. A first name approach from the worker, though still having the connotations of a personal relationship, does not carry the same gender or even sexual overtones as does that approach initiated by a female worker. Unless perhaps, the client is homosexual.

On most occasions the approach from the client will be on a man-to-man basis but there can be a parallel to the child–mother approach when the client projects the worker into the father role of a child–father relationship. The client may then see the worker as the 'father he would have liked to have had' (the most likely), or the 'father he had and didn't like', or even 'hated'. So the client may be dependent, or antagonistic, or waver between both.

When the client does decide to become antagonistic there will be other strands in the background besides the father–son resonances which will be of influence. These may be the teacher–schoolboy, or perhaps even previous worker–client relationships, in additon to a macho-man versus macho-man combatative element.

A multi-cultural society, unlike a single-cultural society (if there are any in the world now), has additional cross-currents of gender assumptions relating to changes of environment, for instance moving from overseas to the UK. Although the two cultures may be different the original assumptions and attitudes are not immediately changed with a change of locale.

This obviously has repercussions for workers in the Personal Services. Workers must learn about, and be sensitive to, the assumptions and attitudes of cultures other than their own. These differences can be significant. For example, it might be quite inappropriate to carry out cross-gender work with clients from particular backgrounds.

It is important for the worker to bear in mind the age of the client and the length of time his/her family has spent in a Western environment. Becoming part of a Western environment can cause considerable culture-conflict between the generations especially when concerning the role of the genders. Workers of the Personal Services may therefore become involved in various capacities, often with a brief to effect a family reconciliation.

When this is to be between a daughter and father, which gender should the worker be? Female, to relate to the daughter? There is a distinct possibility that the female worker will be rejected solely by the traditionalist father on grounds of gender, especially if she tries to persuade him to meet his daughter half-way. Should a male worker be assigned the case? The traditional father will be more likely to initially relate to a man, but he may feel it inappropriate for his daughter to confide in a man. If he is young he may be seen by the father to support his daughter against parental views.

The female client

It is just as unlikely for female clients to have thought deeply or reached any understanding of the deeper aspects of the nature of the relationship between the genders as it is for male clients. Female clients will also naturally approach the worker with assumptions and attitudes based on earlier environments and experiences.

Female client/female worker

There may be an underlying assumption with some female clients that another woman might 'understand' them better because as women they have share experiences. If the worker is older she may become a 'mother-figure' which as well as being a positive role model can have another side. For example, if a teenage client is currently rebelling against her mother she will probably rebel against the worker as well because the two women's roles are perceived as similar. However, the mother may have a positive view of the worker, feeling that the two factors of femaleness and age will mean a shared understanding.

If the worker is considerably younger than the client her views may be dismissed as irrelevant, for example, when discussing child rearing methods, unless she has some external qualification such as nursing which is recognised and accepted by the client. The Social Work qualification is unlikely to be recognised as giving specialised knowledge in the same way a medical qualification would.

However, if the client and younger worker are of a similar age, the worker may be seen more as a knowledgeable sister-figure with shared female experiences and also being of an age to be able to relate to the client's current relationship problems.

Female client/male worker

The male worker will also be perceived by female clients on the basis of his gender and age in relation to hers. The older male worker may be seen as a father-figure especially by a younger female client, with all the resonances of that earlier relationship, and especially as he will be seen to have a certain authority by reason of his role.

There may be adverse repercussions if the female client had earlier been assaulted sexually or physically by her father or some other older male. This may cause an anxiety about one to one office interviews and Home visits which might seem otherwise unaccountable. But greater problems may be caused if the male worker raises this subject with an anxious client. She may find it impossible to discuss what happened between her and the older male, especially if it was her father. She may find a one-to-one setting with a male worker too intimate, even if it is an office. If the worker was wrong in his assumption and there had been no such problems, she may begin to regard him with intense suspicion and wonder what he 'really' meant.

In these situations, there is much to be said for female workers dealing with female clients.

The younger male worker is likely to be viewed in a very different way by the younger female client, especially if she is over school age and he initiates first name terms between them. This will cause confusion to the client because the worker will have created an atmosphere of a personal relationship which she is likely to interpret as friendship. If the worker then has cause to exercise Statutory authority, resentment will be caused and seen as 'betrayal by a friend'.

Cross-gender work

When a task involves cross-gender conflict as in Divorce Court Welfare work for example, then the cross-gender worker may get drawn into the arena. The male worker may be seen by the male

partner as an ally 'against all the women ganging up on me'.
Occasionally he may regard him with suspicion as being, 'an official
who always listens to women's sob stories'.

The female partner may look at him with a mirror-image to the
reason above. 'I must gain his sympathy because he is a man, and his
position gives him influence in the decisions,' or 'I don't trust him
because he is a man like my husband and men always stick together.'

Similar types of thoughts, in reverse order, are likely to apply if
the worker is female.

Workers need to act in such a way that those initial attitudes of the
clients become changed by experiencing relationships with the
worker that are different from those initially assumed. But both
situations present traps for both genders of workers. To fall into any
of them will block the objectivity of the worker and only reinforce the
distrust of the clients.

All cross-gender work is inherently laden with not only the gender
complexities but also underlying sexual connotations. Neither workers nor clients are sexless beings.

In the situations in which they find themselves workers of both
genders are necessarily sympathetic, helpful, resourceful and suppor-
tive people, even though challenging. If they aren't then they cannot
be effective social workers. Clients see themselves as being in need of
some kind of help, at the very least to stay out of custody. After that,
when in a wide variety of situations help is offered and given by a
'kindly' person, emotions of an 'unprofessional' nature can develop
on the part of either or both sides. It is particularly likely when the
worker's attitude is in sharp contrast to the client's previous gender
experience in his/her own environment. For example, if a female
client has a partner who is domineering, contemptuous and aggressive, if not violent, and a male worker who is kindly, empathetic and
helpful.

Not all workers have maintained their professional standards.

If this is perceived or suspected by the client's partner the worker
is likely to become faced with a variety of difficult situations: a threat
to report this to the Agency unless certain things are done or not done
(in effect, blackmail), the partner going to the media with the story, or
a confrontation by that partner in the office or at their home. Such a
confrontation can move rapidly from a verbal argument to physical
violence which, if the worker resists, can make an even better story for
both the media and the partner to capitalise on.

The media have repeatedly demonstrated an eagerness to seize
upon any professional failure of workers in the Personal Services, and
even those of people purporting to be workers. This, in turn, has
created and nurtured a degree of generalised distrust which may spill
over into distrust of a particular worker by some clients and which

may well affect their perception of his/her motives and their interpretation of what s/he says.

Cross-gender co-working

There are clients and there are situations where two workers operating together can forestall some problems developing, provide a more effective service to the client and enhance the safety of both. When the workers are cross-gender rather than single-gender the benefits are greater still.

Clients may provide particular problems by reason of their offences or when their Baseline behaviour shows a propensity to aggression and violence. It is almost axiomatic nowadays that work with sex offenders should be cross-gender co-working whenever that is possible. A violent offender may have committed the offence in particular circumstances that do not normally arise in their life – alternatively of course, aggression and violence may be very much part of their daily life.

In circumstances of family conflict cross-gender co-working is particularly relevant whatever the channel by which the members have come into contact with the Personal Services. On that basis both genders in the family will have someone with whom they can relate. The workers will pool their particular understandings and insights and the possibility of accusations over gender bias or malpractices are much more unlikely, and may even be eliminated altogether. Each of the clients would be likely to see that one is counter-balanced by the other.

Further, there is the inbuilt back-up if problems of potential violence should arise.

All these safeguards especially apply when violence, often between the family partners, is the major reason for contact with the Personal Services.

8 The impact of violence

No worker in any Agency is superhuman. Consequently when a worker is attacked in the course of duty s/he is just as much a 'victim' as any passerby or householder being attacked at random by a violent aggressor. So naturally they will experience just the same feelings and reactions as any other victim. But with some additional ones as well.

During the incident

Shock

Many victims describe their initial feeling during a violent attack as being one of shock and disbelief, especially if violence is outside their normal range of experience. But a person accustomed to 'pub punch-ups' in which s/he is often an active participant, as well as a 'victim', will experience little shock when it happens to them yet again, especially if it is in the same familiar setting. This is because it is all a part of their 'normal' range of experience.

Similarly, at the lighter end of the violence continuum, a worker, unused in his/her personal life to discussions that rapidly degenerate into screaming matches, will experience a measure of shock when the technique is used by a client against them or between clients, whether in the office or on a Home visit, until or unless s/he becomes accustomed to it. To some clients it is part of their 'normal' way of working through any dispute whether it is big or small. But even if that is their norm the worker does not have to sanction or condone it, but rather try to teach his/her clients that there are less disruptive and stressful methods of discussing a problem.

'Shock' can be described as ranging from being 'sharply startled' to being thrown off-balance to the extent of losing control of the situation or, moving more towards the extreme, panicking or a paralysis of action.

One aspect of shock, especially when the violence is towards the heavier end of the continuum, and experienced for the first time, is a horrible sick feeling of 'This can't be happening to *me*!'.

Most people are usually in control of the day-to-day events in their lives, at least to a considerable degree. Workers in the various Agencies are likewise usually in control of their professional interactions with clients too. So when a client takes away a worker's accustomed control by some greater or lesser degree of violence, the shock to the worker is initially all the greater, affecting as it does his/her professional persona as well as his/her personal safety.

Professional concern

This is the factor the professional worker experiences in addition to the normal feelings of being a victim: the question of how his/her colleagues and the Agency's Management will view his/her professional performance and, starting from that, his/her professional competence.

That can cause greater anxiety, not merely over how their chances of promotion may be affected, but over the possibility of Disciplinary Proceedings if the situation is seen by Senior Management as not having been handled professionally, competently and appropriately. In a small survey conducted among the workers of an Agency some years ago 82 per cent expressed anxiety over this possibility.

Legal action by a disgruntled client is always possible and without Management's support the worker's position is even less secure.

Fear

This is the perfectly normal human reaction to danger which is associated with shock to a certain extent. But only to a certain extent, because there can be an anticipatory fear that disappears as the situation sharply deteriorates. At that point there may be no time for fear anyway as the mind concentrates on dealing with the problem.

Many people in the Armed Services have described exactly those processes before and during combat missions.

Case study
One worker, when intervening to protect a wife being attacked by her husband, was grabbed by the throat by the attacker. As he acted in self-defence the thought flashed through his mind of just those consequences if he broke his attacker's little finger in the process of levering it up to break the grip. Even if the police, the Crown Prosecution Service or a jury accepted the plea of self-defence, would that also be the view of a Disciplinary Hearing for Unprofessional Conduct in front of the Management Committee?

Fortunately the client hurriedly released the grip without any of those dire consequences happening!

There are three factors that influence the amount of fear felt:

Self-confidence
This is a feeling that is influenced by lessons learned from experience. As a person grows and develops, being successful in childhood things breeds a belief that more can and will be successfully accomplished. Further successes continue to reinforce that belief and so the child becomes a confident adult. The fact that there are also some failures does not necessarily destroy that belief, though it may be affected. For example, a shattering experience that cannot be coped with will seriously affect it, but bad experiences that are coped with, enhance it.

When facing a new set of situations, training to deal with them will provide a confidence of being able to cope with them in reality. When the first real ones are so coped with, self-confidence is further reinforced in that new area.

For example, a brand-new trainee flyer will be nervous about his/her ability to cope with the new experience of learning to actually pilot an aircraft. The training and then the actual experience of successfully doing it in progressive steps turns the nervous pupil into the confident airline or fighter pilot.

Similarly, the worker coming into the new area of Social Work undergoes training, experiences success in assisting clients and becomes the experienced, confident worker who knows s/he can cope, usually. This question arises though. To what extent do Agencies train their workers to deal with clients who become overtly aggressive and violent? A gap in this aspect of training may well cause a lack of self-confidence when an aggressive or violent situation is encountered.

Equipment
Workers in the Personal Services are not provided with any

equipment for dealing with violent situations beyond an alarm button in their office or a personal alarm which they carry with them. Mobile telephones are not usually supplied to workers, though sometimes higher level administrators are issued with them. They, however, rarely encounter violent clients. In one case, where a child was taken into care for its own safety from potentially very dangerous parents, the workers were equipped with mobile telephones. They testified to a greatly increased feeling of security.

Usually workers' only equipment lies in their casework skills – and any skill in Breakaway, Restraint and Self-Defence techniques in which they may have been trained. If they have had such training, they receive a large boost in self-confidence as a beneficial by-product.

Unexpectedness

There are two aspects to this. Firstly, a worker not anticipating that an attack could ever happen to them. This is part of the ordinary psychological defence mechanism. In reality few people actually expect harm to befall them. But a worker's situation when on duty is different to the norm in that their daily task is to deal with people who are likely to have a higher propensity for violence. With that in mind workers should approach this possibility as they approach crossing a road – being aware but not preoccupied and perennially worried about it. But as a crossing across a busy road causes a heightened awareness, so a worker should exercise increased awareness of the possibility of violence whilst working.

Secondly, a worker not anticipating an attack in this particular interview at this particular time. This can happen to anyone but its likelihood is reduced with adequate training. That training should inculcate an awareness that violence is always a possible experience, teach to watch for the signs that a violent situation may be developing, and how to deal with it when it erupts.

After the incident, the after-effects on the worker

These need to be considered in three time-spans:

Immediate

This is the period lasting for about the ninety minutes that it takes for the level of adrenalin to return to normal after the stimulus (the incident) has ceased. During that period the mood may be one of elation or despondency, or swing from one to the other. Alternatively, if the adrenalin did not rise very high, the mood may remain calm.

Close in time

The night and early morning following the incident. On going to bed the incident, its anxieties and the possibility of future meetings with that violent client may well dominate the worker's thoughts. De-briefing (see below) will assist in putting all those anxieties into perspective. Discussion with his/her partner may or may not help the worker further. It can be frustrating when the partner is unable to truly 'share' the experience, either because s/he is not empathetic or because s/he simply does not understand the working scenario with all its nuances. Or again, because s/he conveys, with or without actually saying so, that s/he believes the worker is making an unnecessary fuss over something that s/he doesn't see as very serious – the results on the worker may not match the violence they have seen on television fiction. S/he may, of course, be indifferent to what has happened to the worker and the repercussions it may have had.

The situation may still be very 'live' in the worker's mind the next morning when it is necessary to go to work again and possibly face the same client again or other clients, inevitably one's colleagues and perhaps enquiries from Senior Management.

Consequently there may be a reluctance to go to work at all.

But that return to work must be done and the sooner the better. Facing fear is the quickest way to break its grip. 'Taking a break' is more likely to aggravate than resolve the problem. Of course, if there have been physical injuries, that break may be inevitable.

Long term

How long term the effects will be will depend on several factors: the seriousness of the injuries, how frightening the incident actually was to the worker or workers involved, whether there was effective debriefing afterwards, the response and support from colleagues and Senior Management and, most importantly, the worker's own emotional responses to having become a 'victim' of criminal violence, i.e. how 'thrown' s/he has been by the incident, whether minimally or seriously.

The need for debriefing

Debriefing is not a simple recounting of the facts of what happened before, during and after the incident. That is reporting, a necessary but a different matter. That has to be done for the client records, for the information of Senior Management and perhaps for the police.

Debriefing is when the people involved in the incident talk to someone, usually the office manager, detailing not only the events but also the worker's own feelings about them. Then there needs to be a devising of better and more successful strategies, if alternative ones are necessary, for dealing with that situation or similar ones in the future. All these elements need to be included for the debrief to be effective in helping the worker to deal with the emotional repercussions, and for it to assist him/her and the whole staff of that office.

The describing of the events while they are still fresh in the mind helps to give a more objective review before the emotions around them colour the memory. It puts them into the correct perspective, with the part that each element played in the total situation.

Describing the feelings experienced helps to ventilate them before the emotions of anxiety, weakness and failure, if there, become repressed and so undermine the worker's self-confidence later. It will help prevent the aggressor taking-on ogre-like proportions in the memory.

When the feelings are of confidence at having dealt with a severe problem successfully, they will be reinforced still further.

The devising of an alternative strategy, if that is needed, will help counteract feelings of helplessness and anxiety about what to do the next time. This promotes the learning by experience factor.

Case study
In one office a mentally disturbed client who was drunk arrived during the lunch-hour when only three secretaries were in the building – a single storey, large, wooden hut. It was the standard practice at lunchtime to lock the office outer door. The door had a sign showing the re-opening time. The client was known as being capable of severe violence – so the staff were well aware of his Baseline behaviour.

He began to kick the door, which was not very strong, demanding admittance even though he did not know if anyone was inside or not. Then he began to howl like a dog.

The secretaries discussed whether to let him in, but decided it would be too dangerous in his present state of mind. They telephoned for the client's own worker but he took 15 minutes to get to the office from where he lived. Just before he arrived the client departed, still howling like a dog, leaving the secretaries shaken but unharmed. Only the door showed the marks of the client's anger.

They discussed the whole situation with the office manager when he arrived shortly afterwards, covering all three aspects of Debriefing. At the end, which took the whole of that Friday afternoon, they all went home.

Having put the events into perspective, off-loaded all the emotions and devised a strategy for future use, the secretaries spent the weekend and returned to the office on the Monday morning quite happily.

It was the office manager who had spent the weekend worrying – about the secretaries and how they were coping!

The need for reporting

Apart from the debriefing, the events will need to be reported to two, perhaps three, sets of people.

The client's record

This is relevant from the viewpoint of office management and will be needed if any legal proceedings such as a prosecution, or an injured worker seeking compensation from the Agency, result. But most importantly, it is produced so that colleagues and future workers with that client are able to form a judgement about the way to interview that client. This is the essential part of gathering information, to be able to make a judgement about that client's Baseline behaviour based on factual information.

It is no help to colleagues or the client him/herself to conceal what happened either out of a wish to be kind to the client, or for the worker to try to hide his/her own mistakes, if indeed there were any.

Many of the clients of the Personal Services need to learn as adults what they have failed to learn as children – that all behaviour brings consequences, and that unpleasant or negative behaviour will bring similar consequences. Learning that, and then, as a result, deciding to modify that behaviour is an essential factor in a person' development.

Senior Management needs to be informed

It is becoming more usual to inform Senior Management, as it is the only way a Headquarters can monitor the scale of the problems caused to workers by violent clients. If they are not told, they will naturally assume that there are no incidents.

At a time when one office manager was trying to convince the Senior Management of his Agency that there was a problem, it was consistently denied because no reports of any had come through. When a course on the subject was finally organised a Senior Manager, who was persuaded to attend, declared shock at the examples given by the workers of their experiences, because none had been reported.

If there has been injury and a claim for compensation sought, Management has to be informed of the events within 24 hours under the Health and Safety at Work Act, otherwise the claim may be invalidated.

Senior Management may also need to be involved if a decision is to be made about banning the client from the premises altogether.

The police

The Agency may have a policy of reporting all serious events to the
police with a view to prosecution, even if they have not been called to
the scene during the incident. To have such a policy is wise because
the individual worker is not then required to make a personal decision
to initiate proceedings which may induce a conflict of values between
his/her personal feelings and those of wanting to 'help' the client. Also
the client is made to realise that the Agency itself will take action to
protect and support its workers.

   In the final analysis of course, an injured worker can refuse to give
evidence against a client, motivated perhaps by kindness, guilt or
possibly fear of reprisals.

9 After violence – after-shock

People's reactions to violence varies greatly. Boxers and wrestlers presumably like it or they would choose some other occupation or sport. Other sports, ranging from karate to rugger, have elements of violence in them but people cheerfully join in and do violence and have violence done to them, though normally only to the levels permitted under the rules.

But in ordinary life, personal violence carries with it elements that sporting violence usually does not, that of malevolence. And, in particular, it is carried out on people who do not want it.

The intensity of the individual's emotional reactions to an attack are obviously influenced by the degree of violence used. But that is not the only factor. Some people are devastated by an attack that others manage to cope with, even if only just, and which others again may simply shrug off.

This is as true for workers in the Personal Services as much as for the general public.

Why is there such a difference in people's reactions?

Fear and anxiety after a sudden attack are normal and to a greater or lesser extent, only to be expected. They are the only human reactions to traumatic events.

There is, I think, a fine but definite distinction that can be drawn between the definitions of 'fear' and 'anxiety', rather than these being different words but meaning exactly the same thing.

'Fear' is more related to a specific person or event. 'Anxiety' is more related to a generalised attitude or emotion, affecting all levels of consciousness. It is not so specific as fear though it can be related to a particular type of person or event.

For example, after an attack by a drunken client there can be a specific *fear* of meeting that individual again but a more generalised *anxiety* could develop about dealing with any and all drunken clients.

How far this will impair the worker functioning will be influenced by several factors:

The victim's own previous experience of violence

This influences not only the degree of shock reaction immediately upon the attack happening but also the later effects. A person who has experienced violence before in their personal life may have learned to cope with it in all the time spans. Another experience may not affect them emotionally to any great extent because of those learned coping mechanisms. A person who has not learned to cope, may have worse reactions because the new experience only serves to reinforce all their old fears, anxieties and emotions.

Training experience

A person who has had training for dealing with aggressive and violent situations is less likely to be 'thrown' by one. An SAS trooper is not going to be as upset by a thug taking a punch at him as a person who has never encountered physical violence before.

The in-born resilience factor

Some people appear to possess this to a greater degree than others. It is not the psychopathic indifference often found in persistent violent offenders but the capacity to deal with fairly extreme situations.

Dealing with the aftermath

Most people adjust to most situations without needing any outside help. But for some, after an experience of violence, perhaps several of them, an introjected worry about putting themselves in that situation again may develop, a fear of meeting that particular client, anxiety over meeting any similar clients or meeting any clients at all, or even going to the office. Effective debriefing will help resolve that problem before it arises of course, but for some it will not eliminate it altogether.

That worker may need the help of a counsellor to deal with the anxiety and an Agency should have made provision for that help to be available. Working with potentially violent clients after an incident can develop from an anxiety into mild or severe phobia. For a worker in Social Work where that type of client or situation is always around, the effects will lie somewhere along a continuum running from stressful, through undermining, to disabling.

The basic premises

Anxiety gives rise to both feelings and thoughts, which are closely bound together and influence each other. Both need to be tackled to deal effectively with the anxiety.

There are four basic premises or assumptions that need to be fully accepted and then adopted in practice.

Confronting
      The way to conquer fear and anxiety is to confront (not avoid) that which causes them. Taking care to avoid the causer seems a way to resolve the problem but the area of avoidance action is likely to grow until the anxious worker avoids not only the type of incident or person that was the causer but situations and people that impinge or verge on the original experience.

For example, a person injured by a drunken client may initially take action to avoid that client when s/he is drunk; then when s/he is sober; then any client who is drunk; then any client who may be drunk even if they are only noisy.

Avoidance action only reinforces the lack of self-confidence that underlies the feelings. Confronting the causer can be done in various 'safe' ways which will enhance self-confidence, and so the worker can be emboldened to confront the causer in all situations.

In the example used above, the client should be interviewed, perhaps several times, when sober, with another worker present to give support to the injured worker. Then s/she should be interviewed when sober, by that worker alone; then with self-confidence growing, the worker continues with the client.

Understand, and accept, that a feeling of fear is a normal human reaction to a 'threat'. Fear, in the face of a powerful threat that is believed cannot be coped with, has been essential for the survival of people throughout the ages. So the 'flight' bit of the 'flight-fight' syndrome is not the reaction of cowardice, it is simply being human.

It is *how* that natural fear is handled that marks the brave person.

Learn to ride the inrush of feelings of fear until they diminish – the feelings are partly associated with the biochemical reactions of the body itself, i.e. the secretion of adrenalin. As the mind becomes accustomed to the fear-inducing situation, the level of adrenalin begins to subside so the first acute feelings diminish.

Learn to control the negative thoughts of fear by using the more positive thoughts of one's own capability or capacity for dealing with the threat. For the basic *thought* underlying fear and anxiety is the belief that one is incapable of coping with the threat whatever it may be and whether the anxiety is based on reality or not. Because a fear-causer can become ogre-sized in the imagination.

The basic techniques

Once the basic premises have been accepted it is then possible to move on to dealing with the fear or anxiety syndrome itself, recognising and accepting that this is a problem that really can be solved.

A counsellor (or a partner who really knows how to help and support) is really essential for this. It is totally ineffective to let the thoughts surge around unformulated. *Thinking* about the problem does not exteriorise it.

There are two basic techniques for doing this.

Desensitisation

This technique is the gradual facing of the threat, which is steadily increased as each stage is learned to be coped with. In real life it is difficult to create an actual sequence of gradually developing physical threats from clients, so one of two methods has to be adopted.

(a) *Using fantasy.* The worker takes a physically relaxed position on a bed, in a comfortable chair with head support, or even on the traditional psychiatrist's couch. It is only necessary to be comfortable and physically relaxed.

Once comfortable, steadily and consciously tense, s/he should then relax all the muscles of the body, beginning at the toes, working up the legs, body, neck and face, then up the arms from the fingers.

Once fully relaxed the workers should then visualise, feel and describe in detail a situation that generates a mild feeling of threat consistent with the circumstances that cause the anxieties s/he is trying to resolve. For one person that could be a noise in a distant office for which the worker has and feels no responsibility at all to deal with. For another it will be an interview with an awkward but known non-violent client. For another it will be something else again.

Whatever is perceived by the worker as a potential threat, will cause an anxiety response as s/he 'lives' the situation. If there is no such response, s/he should bring the scene closer in space or upgrade the potential threat.

While the anxiety is being felt, s/he should devise realistic strategies for dealing with the situation and use them to describe in the fantasy how to deal with that anxiety-provoking situation. The process should be repeated many times.

The feeling of anxiety will diminish over time because of the level of adrenalin dropping and because there is an actual and practical working out of how to deal with that situation. This becomes, in effect, a training session which actually increases capability. The worker, understanding, accepting and introjecting that concept actually increases his/her skills in this area, which in turn increases self-confidence, which then, in turn, increases his/her actual capability.

Once the anxiety has gone from that situation, which may take a little time, move on to a closer, more threatening situation, and repeat the process.

Over time this repeated pattern will result in a developing feeling of confidence about not just being able to barely cope with, but to deal successfully with similar situations using the strategies that have been devised. When these are tested in real life and the strategies used successfully, the self-confidence becomes all the firmer because the 'training' has worked and the anxiety level reduced again.

(b) *Using role play.* The worker should design with the counsellor a situation that poses mild threat (as in the fantasy technique) and in that planned design include strategies for dealing with it.

This is acted out in role play. The anxiety response is likely to be greater for a given situation than in the fantasy technique, for it is obviously more real. But the anxiety response will reduce more rapidly and self-confidence build more rapidly precisely for that same reason.

Once that level of anxiety is dealt with, move on to the next stage of increased threat until those levels are dealt with in turn.

Flooding

This technique is more drastic but is likely to be more effective more quickly. The actual situation that caused the problem is relived as fully as possible.

(a) *Using fantasy.* As in the desensitisation technique bodily relaxation is important. Once that is achieved, the actual incident is relived describing to the counsellor the physical events and the emotional reactions that were experienced in all their detail. Not once only, but many times until the feelings of anxiety diminish and go.

One writer has advocated that this should be done for two hours rather than one!

The point is that the experience, which is after all an unusual rather than everyday one, is put into its proper perspective in the worker's mind.

Strategies are devised to deal with the situation and, at this stage, the experience is described again to the point where these new strategies are introduced.

Particularly with this method an abreaction (a re-experiencing of the total emotional responses) may well occur. It is a helpful and perhaps necessary cathartic experience which releases the previously repressed emotions.

Case study

A boy who had had a traumatic experience during World War II began suffering nightmares in which he saw flashes of light coming from his bedroom as he went up the stairs to bed. Finally, after having this nightmare three nights in a row he refused to go to bed and for a long time he wouldn't give the reason. Eventually he described the nightmare, shaking and crying with all the horror of the terror that the nightmare gave him. His mother listened silently, then talked of the time he had been buried under the rubble of the bombed building with the lights of the rescuers causing flashes across his face as they searched. By reliving that experience, talking about it and so exteriorising the emotions in a cathartic outburst, the terror was released and he no longer suffered that nightmare.

Essentially this parallels the debriefing session but with the additional complications of a repressed emotions factor which the debriefing session is designed to prevent.

(b) *Using role play.* The worker should recreate with the counsellor the actual incident that occurred as far as may be possible. Obviously any physical injuries do not need to be re-inflicted!

The same process of repetition and devising of strategies to deal with the situation are gone through, but the amount of repetition needed is slashed.

In the incident when the worker was grabbed by the throat by a client, there was no debriefing and the emotional repercussions were undermining and to some extent, disabling for a long time afterwards.

Finally, in a group setting a full description of the incident was given followed by a re-enactment, though the grip on the throat was not so hard. A repeat, but this time using another technique to break the grip, helped in the therapeutic process.

During that process what happened was that there was a degree of abreaction, a strategy devised and refined, which was then rehearsed.

And the anxieties around that incident diminished which then had a 'knock-on' effect on the emotional responses to other acute situations.

The timing of giving help

The timing of giving this help is important and to this end Agencies should build into their systems a debriefing and counselling process for workers who become involved in a serious incident. The earlier this help is given, the less time there is for the natural stress reactions to develop into a phobic state. The stress reaction will then be dealt with while the incident and its attendant emotions are at the forefront of the mind and there would be less time for any repression to take place. This enables the problem to be resolved more easily, speedily and effectively.

Though these techniques will help resolve specific anxieties they cannot, and will not, eliminate all feelings of stress that naturally arise when a worker is faced with a potential or actual violent situation. But that stress will be much reduced by the enhancement of the worker's confidence in him/herself and their skills in having devised useful strategies for dealing with those situations.

In the majority of cases an effective, speedy debriefing will be all that is necessary to prevent these problems developing at all.

10 Why not run anti-violence courses?

Inappropriate techniques

Some years ago I was discussing with a group of office managers the need to treat seriously the problem of the aggression and violence that was sometimes shown by some clients to workers. During the discussion I covered the provisions that I saw as being necessary – making buildings safer and more secure, devising safer policies and practices and providing courses in restraint and self-defence techniques for the staff that wanted them.

The response from one office manager was an immediate, blanket and total refusal to countenance any and all such Courses. Even though eighty-two per cent of main-grade workers who had responded to a two-page questionnaire I had circulated, wanted them.

When faced with this figure she retorted, 'Well let them go and take karate courses themselves then.'

This answer begs three questions:

1   Is karate the right kind of system to learn for dealing with a wide range of situations that can range from a single punch, through a short flurry of pushing or punching, to a potential or actual lethal attack?
2   Are there not more appropriate techniques around rather than just those that injure, for dealing with the Agencies' clients?

3   Is it not the Agencies' responsibility to teach appropriate
    techniques to its workers for dealing with its clients, in this as
    well as in all other situations?

Karate, of which there are several styles, is a particular martial art
that employs a pattern of kicks and blows delivered sharply and with
force. When practiced as a sport its practitioners are well-padded, but
even so injuries can be inflicted accidently. One person I heard of had
his jaw broken.

When used in a self-defence situation, as there will be no padding-
up, it will inevitably cause injury, perhaps permanent injury. A chop
to the side of the neck, or a kick in the ribs or kneecap are not meant
to be gentle taps in karate.

A second problem is the small amount of space that is actually
available in the average sized office would prevent a number of the
techniques effectively being used.

And karate does not cover breakaway or restraint techniques
which after all, is not what karate is concerned with.

So altogether karate itself does not make a good 'fit' with our role,
the variety of situations we face, nor, in fact, the personal values of
many who work in the Personal Services.

Appropriate techniques

Courses that do provide the appropriate variety of techniques are:

- Breakaway courses,
- Restraint courses,
- Self-Defence courses.

Though all these could be covered in one course, it would be very
intensive, take considerable time and, probably, be trying to cram in
too much, especially if time is to be given to practice which is, of
course, essential. The courses should form a natural progression,
though each is complete in itself.

Breakaway techniques

These are, rather obviously, those techniques that enable a person
who has been seized by an attacker to break free. They cover escaping
from a grip on the throat, hair or clothing from front, side or rear.
Though essentially defensive, some of the methods can involve
hurting the aggressor. Once free the defender either escapes or, if in a
worker–client situation, continues to try to talk the situation down.

Restraint techniques

These are a grade up on breakaway, inasmuch as the defender, having broken free, if that was needed, grabs the aggressor in a hold that prevents the attack continuing until the aggressor calms down or more back-up arrives. The techniques cover either a hold that prevents physical movement in itself or, by inflicting considerable pain if the attack continues, makes the aggressor desist.

A problem with these techniques can be that a certain amount of strength is needed by the defender, especially if the aggressor is more powerful physically than the defender and also if s/he has some knowledge of these techniques him/herself. So the attempt to gain and maintain a Restraint hold may result in a wrestling match which exacerbates the problem rather than resolving it.

Self-defence techniques

This term can be used to include the two previous courses but more properly, as referred to here, should be regarded as a separate group. The techniques are those that stop an attack by disabling the aggressor temporarily or permanently.

To some this will cut across their personal values and beliefs as they refuse to cause injury to another for any reason whatsoever. And it is the possibility of permanent injury being caused that gives the greatest concern to the Senior Managements of Agencies. They fear the Agency being sued by disabled and angry clients. That fear is becoming an increasingly realistic one as people are beginning to follow the American trend of seeking financial compensation whenever possible.

The reality of life is that safe facilities and good prevention policies and practices will mean that most potentially volatile situations simply will not happen. Even more will be prevented by aggressors being 'talked down' by the skills of the workers. But it is also a reality of life that some situations will occur where the worker is attacked despite all these preventative measures being employed, no matter how good they are, either by reason of the circumstances or because of the type of client concerned.

Questions concerning the provision of courses

In the past three questions have been asked fairly regularly about the provision of such courses by Agencies.

Should attendance be compulsory?

To impose compulsory attendance at courses for workers after qualification is still fairly rare, though it seems to be increasing for some topics such as Race and Gender issues. More usually workers apply to go on the courses they wish to attend themselves or that are suggested by their Line Manger. There is no reason why these courses should be made compulsory, only that they are advisable.

A second problem for managers who might wish to make them compulsory is that for some workers anything connected with violence or physical resistance is against their personal scale of values. In the questionnaire mentioned earlier, one respondent to the question, 'Should Management provide courses in restraint and self-defence techniques?' replied, 'No. And if they did I would refuse to attend.'

As some workers feel this is a moral rather than a simple practical issue, their values must influence management strictures.

Doesn't the need for constant practice to maintain speed of response impose too much strain on limited training budgets?

Yes, but there are two factors about these skills which should be made.

The instinct of 'fight-flight' reactions to threat does produce a speedy, almost automatic response – unless the other response of 'freezing' happens of course! A learned skill of self-defence will cause the more likely response to be one of action rather than freezing. There is therefore already a built-in speed factor to some extent.

The situation being prepared for is not one of unarmed combat against a trained adversary. The clients like that are very few and a violent confrontation with such a person is likely to be beyond the capacity of the average worker in the Personal Services. The violent clients that are the norm are more those of the 'rough and tumble' variety, even if fighting is part of their usual or even customary way of life. Any skills they have are rarely the result of training, more of experience of schoolboy type fights, even if considerably more vicious.

Also we are not speaking of unarmed combat but self-defence. The two are very different.

So constant practice to hone speed is not really necessary. While frequent practice would be the ideal, it is not essential for this purpose.

Won't the courses make workers over confident and more ready to use violence excessively themselves?

These statements are clearly and directly critical of workers themselves. They imply that such courses will cause workers to fail to use their Social Work skills fully before moving into the area of violence themselves. This is not unlike the reason Senior Officers gave for initially refusing to provide British combat pilots with parachutes in World War 1, i.e. that the pilots would abandon their flying skills, and aircraft, too soon if they had them!

If these concerns of Senior Managements are valid and based on clear assessment of the workers they employ then one must question why they should have selected, employed and retained those workers. They don't seem to trust them!

Furthermore, we are speaking not of workers initiating violence, but being given the opportunity to acquire skills to defend themselves if and when violence is already being used against them. People are not violent because they have been given some training but because they are violent people. Good training teaches self-control and so militates against techniques or skills being used excessively.

The content of courses

Courses in breakaway, restraint and self-defence techniques should teach just a few methods (not a plethora which may get mixed-up and be more easily forgotten) and give space and time for as much practice as possible in the few methods that are taught. That practice will reinforce as well as develop skills in their use, and in turn will allow a reaction-response to form that switches on when a threat situation develops. The confidence of the worker in his/her ability to deal with the more extreme situations should they arise will then increase. This increased self-confidence will help them in the use of their Social Work skills and so keep the violent situations to their lowest possible level.

11 Who should trouble-shoot?

The Personal Services deal with many people who have been in prisons or Young Offender Institutions for serious violence offences including murder. Murderers, after serving a greater or lesser time in custody, are usually released on Licence which is supervised in the community for a period of years and which can be extended for any period up to the time the Licencee dies. Though that Licence is almost always supervised by the Probation Service, other Agencies will inevitably be involved from time to time with that client. They will usually be the Social Security, the Social Services, Housing and possibly the psychiatric services, such as the Community Psychiatric Nurses, who only deal with the more obvious clients who may pose a threat. Other seriously violent people, who may not have been prosecuted, may be released to the care of Social Services Departments.

Those who have committed less serious violence offences than murder will be discharged either on parole or licence at some point partway through the sentence that was imposed, unless it was less than 12 months. Those who have committed violence offences but instead of going to prison receive Community sentences are also supervised under various Orders.

All the Custodial Institutions, to a greater or lesser degree, have a Control and Restraint (C and R) team who have been trained how to physically restrain offenders at any time while they are in custody, either when they act violently by themselves or in the company of others in a riot situation. There are, of course, larger numbers of violent or potentially violent offenders in any one place at any one time in a custodial situation than is likely to be in a Personal Services office at any one time. So a C and R team is more necessary in a custodial situation.

But all too often there is no one at all in a Personal Services office who has been properly trained in any of the restraint techniques, who can trouble-shoot if or when a problem arises from those ex-custodial offenders who have now become their clients back in the community. The clients may have called as casual visitors who become obstreperous in the Waiting area or an office, or they may have become regular clients.

The location of the problem can play a part in deciding who should deal with it. If the problem occurs in a worker's office the type of Incident Alarm fitted also becomes a factor.

The Audible alarm system sounding throughout the office building is likely to be pressed only in extreme cases, when violence is actually happening and a C and R type of mass response is needed. The Silent alarm system allows for a variable range of action and can be an early signal, when a different type of response is needed from the C and R mass rush.

If the problem is in the Waiting Area either type of response may be needed.

The best choice for trouble-shooters?

The young male worker

If he is physically large and muscular, he would seem the ideal choice if a C and R type of response is needed or where a measure of controlling intimidation is called for. But in most Personal Services he is unlikely to have had any training in those techniques at all, as very few Agencies at present do provide that training. Also he is likely to be one of the less experienced workers and so may not be so used to handling this type of situation in the ways more usually appropriate to the Personal Services.

A young male worker who was of large build and had a strong personality commented that he was the person always sent to deal with any obstreperous clients in the Waiting Area. At the time he was telling this he had not been called on to assist with an in-office problem. His earlier experience of working in a voluntary hostel had stood him in good stead but he felt he was not really experienced enough in Probation work to have this role so consistently thrust upon him. Nor had he had any training in Restraint techniques – or any others. The first specific training for dealing with aggressive clients was in fact the course in which he was then participating. He was also finding that aggressive clients were being allocated to him to work with.

The big young male worker may well be regarded, by an already aggressive and/or troublesome client, especially if he too is young and male, as a challenger to be faced down, unless the worker's and client's relative sizes and personality forcefulness are so different as to cause the client to feel intimidated and to back off quickly.

If he does not then the problem may be compounded rather than resolved. That had not yet happened to this young worker but he was concerned that a situation of this sort could arise so he wanted to be better equipped to handle things appropriately.

The female worker

There is a belief that female workers are the best people to deal with an aggressive male client even if he is an unknown casual caller in the Waiting Area. Sometimes the comment used to justify this is 'The aggressive male client won't hit a female worker.'

The reasoning (if such a word can be used of this line of thought) behind this is to be wondered at!

The actual number of women who are hit by aggressive men is only gradually becoming known. But it has been common knowledge for centuries that men do hit women. The assumption that a female worker would somehow be exempt from that behaviour seems to be based on the fact that she is female rather than a worker. But it can be this very factor of gender that makes some men turn on women. Then the fact she is a worker is irrelevant.

The other comment sometimes made is, 'Women can talk aggressive men down better than a man.' That comment again is essentially based on the worker's gender though this is coupled with an assumption about relative levels of casework skills between the genders for which there is no evidence. Should the person making that comment be challenged it clearly cannot be substantiated as a generalisation.

The female worker will not present a male 'challenger' situation to the aggressive male client as a male worker may, but instead may present a handy 'female victim' instead.

The age factor of the worker is never mentioned in this context but those who have this view would usually mean, it seems, the more mature female worker rather than the younger.

A young worker, male or female, will be likely to feel a need to prove his/her competence to his/her colleagues, to demonstrate that s/he can deal with difficult situations and so is 'reliable' and 'one of the team'. S/he will also feel a pressure to prove him/herself to the office manager, again that s/he is competent, professional and reliable. Because at that point of his/her service s/he will be concerned about getting a good evaluation or appraisal which will be important, not only for the immediate good feeling, but for his/her future career. This carries the corollary of anxiety over the outcome if s/he is seen as 'failing' or 'mishandling the situation'. Being a young person the anxieties surrounding that idea and the spectre of disciplinary action is likely to loom large.

Quite obviously, the views about female workers is based on sexist stereotyping which claims men don't hit women and see women having a prime role in society as peacemakers. The Personal Services should have moved away from these stereotypes which are manifestly inaccurate, and yet they are still heard.

An assumption is often made that the aggressive client will always be male. While the likelihood is higher it is by no means always so. Aggressive clients can be mature or young women. This introduces a factor that must alter the emphasis on the gender element of the choice of worker to deal with the problem, unless that gender element is removed from the decision altogether

The office manager

By reason of his/her position in the office, i.e. being the senior person by role, the office manager of either gender is liable to be expected by the rest of the staff to take on the task. If s/he passes it back by delegation, especially to a worker who has not been given adequate and appropriate training for that task, there is likely to be resentment, both from the worker him/herself and from the worker's colleagues, that the office manager is not fulfilling his/her responsibilities and is simply passing the buck. However, if the office manager has ensured that the designated trouble-shooter has had full training and is an experienced worker, then it will be more likely that it will be felt that s/he has acted appropriately.

But this begins to smack of having a 'guard' in Personal Services offices which is hardly what is needed at the present time.

So most commonly, the emphasis will swing back to the office manager to deal with the problem situations when back-up is required, wherever that is.

Increasingly, across the range of Personal Services, the office manager is becoming more of an administrator than a practicing worker, even if s/he was a worker before being appointed a manager. The problem then arises that the manager loses touch with clients, and over a period of time becomes more remote from that day-to-day work and then becomes unrealistic in expectations of clients and workers. To then suddenly be pitched into a highly emotional aggressive situation threatening to get totally out of hand at any moment, is not only alarming but it may not be handled as well as it might be. Again though the manager may have been an experienced worker s/he is not likely to have received any training in any of the appropriate techniques of breakaway or restraint. The difficulty may well be worse if the manager has only ever been an administrator and never a practicing worker. In that event the Senior Caseworker (if there is one) is likely to be a more appropriate person to provide back-up.

In many of the smaller offices the manager, though being primarily an administrator, may be handling clients in a variety of situations on a regular basis. In that event s/he, being an experienced worker and maintaining client-contact, together with the authority of that role, is likely to be the most appropriate person to be the trouble-shooter.

And most probably the other workers will be pleased for him/her to have the task.

12 Children's and young people's homes

The population of children in Residential care has shrunk considerably over the years, from 39,600 in 1980 to 13,200 in 1990 of which 10,490 were in Local Authority Homes. This is partly a reflection of the overall drop of children in care generally from 95,300 in 1980 to 65,500 in 1990. But it also reflects the movement of children into foster homes rather than keeping them in Residential Homes.

The result is that the Residential Homes now provide care for the more difficult youngsters, many of whom have 'failed' in one or more foster placements, or those who may be between placements or cannot be placed. I use the term 'youngster' to cover the whole age range as it is hardly appropriate to classify 16 and 17 year olds as 'children'.

The youngsters are generally at the older end of the scale, the highest percentage being 16 year olds, then 15 year olds, 17 year olds and 14 year olds. These account for 70 per cent of all in residential care, they have more problems that are judged as 'serious' and tend to be those with long histories of disturbance or neglect, or with behavioural problems.

Staff that are mostly untrained look after these often disturbed and disruptive adolescents. The most recent national statistics (surveyed for 'Children in Public Care 1991') showed that nearly 70 per cent of staff were unqualified and 26.3 per cent had been in the post for under two years. Of the Officers in Charge, 79 per cent had some form of

Social Work qualification, but fewer than 50 per cent Assistant
Officers in Charge had any qualification. However, the Training
Support Programme (Child Care) had given some training in general
child care to 7,600 Residential staff in 1989/90, with 6,000 more
anticipated for 1990/91.

Consequently the most seriously disturbed and disruptive youngsters in their mid-teens are being cared for by the least well-trained and
qualified Social Workers. Those who have worked in Residential care
for several years know that this has always been a problem, but the
youngsters now in their care are the more difficult ones.

The Residents

All the youngsters will be in the Home because of family breakdown
of some kind. It may be because the parents are divorced or separated
and are neither able or willing to care for the youngster/s, a single
parent may have been unable to cope with his/her situation any
longer, or the youngster's own behaviour has disrupted the family life
for too long. S/he may have come from a multi-problem family.

S/he may have experienced sexual abuse and seen violence
between the parents, possibly inflicted on other children and have
experienced it him/herself. There may well have been failure to attend
school, solvent/drug/alcohol abuse, self-mutilation and perhaps
suicide attempts, whether gestures or genuine attempts. S/he would
be likely to have experienced rejection, perhaps many times, from
parents, foster parents or other carers, at least partly due to his/her
own behaviour.

There may have been criminal offences which may have resulted
in a Caution or perhaps No Further Action, or have gone to court.
There is often a degree of violence in his/her school history, day-to-
day lives or offending. The cause for that may well have been the
result of experiencing that pattern of behaviour with their parents.
The youngster assumes that is the way people do live and it becomes
his/her norm.

At the age of the majority of these youngsters (14–17 years) they
should normally be at the stage of growing independence and
establishing themselves as independent adults. These are the times
that youngsters are beginning to resent, and sometimes reject, the
authority of others and to resent the limitations that parental figures
still impose upon them, even while they are being gradually loosened.
However, because of their emotional reactions to their family
breakup, their having been rejected themselves perhaps several times
before, the usual inhibiting ties of family affection just aren't there.
Perhaps they have not been there for many years. The examples these

youngsters may have seen and learned from are those of selfishness and 'grab whatever you can as soon as you can'. They may be either streetwise and tough or undermined and vulnerable.

As these factors draw together, their poor life experiences and their developmental milestones, the situation can be potentially explosive, both within themselves and against others. Anything can trigger the explosion.

As with any group of youngsters of these ages, when put together in close proximity, there will be jockeying for leadership positions. It happens in all kinds of situations even where there is a structured group with designated roles. So inevitably this pattern will emerge in Residential Homes as well, but with an edge that is not so usual in other settings by reason of the backgrounds and norms of the youngsters involved.

The rivalries between the youngsters will take various forms. Sometimes there will be high pressure as two strong-minded youngsters both try to dominate the situation. This can become intense as they seek to build a power-base of supporters from the other youngsters by persuasion, pressure, bullying or bribes. At some point the rivals may have a confrontation between themselves which is likely to become physical. This kind of rivalry has repercussions of tension, anxiety and excitement which effectively prevents a calm atmosphere and often results in a level of violence, with resulting probems for the workers.

A single youngster who has the 'power position' alone and unchallenged may hold the Home at an apparent level of calm if s/he chooses to do so, though that is more likely to be because the others are afraid of him/her rather than the kindness of his/her disposition.

But in the same circumstances, if s/he is determined to be disruptive to the workers s/he can lead the rest along causing a multitude of problems. These may be centred round a host of petty disruptions from refusals to carry out reasonable instructions, to wrecking furniture or the Home itself – windows are often a favourite target. The disruption can then spiral as other youngsters try to outdo each other to gain status or the favour of the leader.

It may be that the only way to deal with that situation is to remove the leader to another Home if that is possible, though that may only serve to transfer the problem rather than resolve it. Sometimes though, suddenly losing his/her power-base of support, and becoming the 'new boy' or 'new girl' at a place that already has its relationships network in place in which s/he does not figure, can mute the leader. How long that lasts depends mostly on the youngsters already there and the strengths of their existing relationships network.

The problem of weapons

Youngsters of these higher age groups often have a liking for weapons.
If necessary they may try to manufacture them.

> **Case study**
> A younger boy stole half-a-dozen table knives from the drawer where
> they were kept with the forks and spoons. His intention was to try to
> put an effective cutting edge on them and distribute them round his
> 'gang'. He failed because he couldn't find a suitable sharpening stone
> and he was caught with them.

A prison takes steps to ensure no weapons are around, plastic
utensils are used wherever there is not going to be close supervision.
But the ordinary Residential Home for youngsters is meant to be a
'home' in the usual sense of the word, not an impersonal institution.
Consequently the type of utensils normally found at home are used –
and naturally enough some of them can be used as weapons if someone
is determined enough to do so. Pool cues, though perhaps not
regularly found in the average home, can make excellent weapons to
either jab with or use as a club. Snooker balls can be dangerous when
thrown.

In addition to those makeshift weapons, some youngsters will be
in the habit of carrying knives, not necessarily an ordinary small
penknife, but one of the more dangerous varieties. The possession of
these is likely to be concealed for as long as possible by the youngsters,
either in their clothing, in their personal possessions or in their rooms.

The areas in the home

A Residential Home can be divided into four areas, each of which
creates different safety or security problems.

The office

Every Home needs its administrative area because it will have a fair
sized budget and staff. Efficient administration is essential for the
smooth running of the Home so that what is required for the
youngsters is always there. Just as with an office in the field, a level of
security is needed, perhaps more, because money belonging to the
Home and probably to the youngsters will be kept there. In addition
there will be small items of office equipment, easily transportable with
a ready sale if taken by a youngster.

That, together with staff premises, should be the only place that requires what is called 'official' security, because those are the only 'official' parts of the building. The rest is essentially the home of the youngsters.

Domestic areas

These are the kitchen and storerooms. There are likely to be rules about going into those places (or the larder might be raided continuously!) but whether this should be secured will depend on the particuar Home. An important point to be borne in mind when making that decision is that the kitchen holds many potential weapons. Open access means they might disappear. But, on the other hand, in an ordinary home they are not locked away and establish- ments do try to provide as home-like an environment as possible.

Shared areas

These are the dining room, games room, TV room, library and quiet rooms. There may be rules about the times of the use of some of these or there might be none. Clearly a factor in these decisions will be the size of the Home and the number and type of youngsters it takes. Usually the fewer rules there are the better as in an ordinary home. If the youngsters are free to use the rooms, with responsible freedom, without intrusive supervision by staff, the atmosphere is likely to be more relaxed all round, which helps to keep tension low.

Personal areas

It is important to youngsters of these ages to have space that they can call their own. Ideally it should be a room about which they can feel some degree of ownership and preferably that they can lock them- selves. At least they should have a lockable cupboard to which they have the key.

The problems arise over the degree of privacy.

How often conflicts arise between teenagers and their parents over the 'state' in which they keep their rooms! Clothes everywhere! Books, papers and records scattered around the floor and never tidied away. The bed rarely or never made. Posters of all kinds pinned up on the walls.

Many parents despair and bemoan the way the youngsters will 'turn out' if they are not dragooned into more tidy habits. And the youngsters, with a determination to 'hold their territory' refuse to listen, insist they like the room the way it is – and anyway there are far more important things to think about and do than tidying up a room! Anyway, it will only get untidy again. Most parents, unless they are gluttons for punishment, will retire in defeat when their youngster suggests that they simply shut the door on his/her room and leave it the way s/he wants it and that they should keep the rest of the house tidy if they want it that way.

The situation is different in a Residential Home to a major degree. All too often the youngsters have come from a chaotic background with a chaotic lifestyle of their own. Some standards may well need to be taught. But the privacy factor is still important to those youngsters and needs to be put carefully balanced.

A complicating factor though, is that the type of youngster in Residential Homes may have been involved in or still be involved in solvent/drug/alcohol abuse, or be concealing weapons. The difficulty is whether the possibility that such things might be hidden in their rooms or cupboards over-rides his/her quite natural and legitimate desire for a degree of privacy.

A compromise is that normally the privacy is given, staff always knock on the door before entering and searches are only made when there are grounds for suspicion, and this is done only with the youngster present. The problem then becomes one of definition. What are 'reasonable grounds for suspicion?'.

Care and control

The Children Act 1989 indicates that the 'primary duty of the local authority is to safeguard and promote the welfare of the child who is being looked after' (Section 22 (3)(b)). This encompasses the two elements of care and control. Both are dependant on and influence each other. A 'caring' ethos brings its own controls to bear on those who feel they are genuinely cared for. Understood and accepted controls help bring the stability that enables caring to flourish and be reciprocated by the youngsters.

It has to be accepted that a Residential Home can never be a real home to youngsters, though for long-stay ones it can take on many of the characteristics of familiarity and 'acclimatisation' that almost makes it one. But there are usually too many youngsters there of a similar age and too great a number of staff who work shift patterns. They all may be kindly and caring, but it is not possible to relate to a youngster when working shift patterns in the way that a good parent relates to his/her own child, with the constancy and presence of normal family life. The workers and the youngsters know it is not that kind of relationship.

Residential Homes provide, at the most basic level, shelter, security and food for the youngsters. There may be planned preparation for independent adult life either exclusively for those in that age group in a spread-age-band Home, or for everyone in a Home where all the youngsters are of that age.

Workers of all grades and types of job in a Home need to possess and present a caring attitude, in addition to providing the basic elements. A 'key worker' to whom a youngster can relate most and who takes a special interest in him/her, can be very important and the influence last long after the contact has come to an end.

Case study

A boy spent eighteen months in various hospitals from the time he was 9 years of age. He had previously been fostered out for three years many miles from his own home which had not been a happy time for him and during which he had seen his mother twice and his father once. In one hospital he formed a closer relationship with one staff nurse than he had done with anyone for all those years. The memory of that stayed with him long afterwards, even when he had returned to his parents who by then were virtual strangers to him.

Those kinds of relationships, especially when reciprocated, make control much easier and simpler. But not all youngsters do respond in that way, which may be due to a 'testing out' of the 'caring', but on the other hand they may not have that motivation at all but are simply being destructive.

Other controls then become necessary, not only for that youngster's sake but for the others living there, those sharing the Home with the disruptive youngster even if they are not being drawn into his/her web of influence.

After the trauma of the Pindown Enquiry in Staffordshire in 1990 there was a period of uncertainty in many quarters as to what controls were permissible.

Basically Pindown was a method devised to deal with, and to control and discipline, youngsters who were considered to be particularly disruptive. Clothes, company and even use of the bathrooms were considered privileges. These were removed and had to be earned through behaviour as specified by 'contract'. All youngsters were subject to Review Meetings when they were 'confronted' with their 'failures to meet their contract'. In 'Full' or 'Total' Pindown the measures were increased in severity. The isolation, at times applied for very many days, and the system had traumatic effects on the youngsters. It came in for great criticism because of the severity imposed on young children and for its traumatic effects.

Not dissimilar programmes have been used at times to treat drug addicts, but people in those programmes were adults, and even they found it traumatic.

For many years before Pindown a number of Residential Homes

had used what was called a 'cool down' room, into which a youngster would be put when in an uncontrolled state and not paying any heed to the attempts to talk down the situation. A watch was kept and as soon as they were in a suitable frame of mind to participate in discussion to resolve the problem, they rejoined the others. The method was not used as a punishment but as a 'hold' and only lasted for a short period of time.

There are now specific Regulations of what methods of control are banned and what are allowed in the Children's Homes Regulations 1991.

The Prohibited Measures (Regulation 8) covers:

- Any form of corporal punishment
- Any deprivation of food or drink
- Any restrictions on visits
- Any requirement for a child to wear particular clothes
- Use or witholding of medication
- Intentional deprivation of sleep
- Imposition of fines, but not reparation
- Any intimate physical examination.

Under Section 25 of the Children Act 1989 the physical restriction of liberty by locking youngsters up, in Homes other than the duly authorised Secure Accommodation Units, is forbidden. The youngsters may be told they cannot go out but if they disobey and go they cannot be locked in and cannot be physically prevented from leaving in general. However it may be possible if there are good grounds for believing that it would not be in his/her best interests. At this point of time it needs to be said that clearer guidance on this point is required because moves to physically prevent a youngster from leaving could well result in violence being used on the workers trying to carry that out.

Permitted Measures (Children Act 1989 Guidance and Regulations Volume 4. Residential Care) covers:

- Approval and rewards
- Verbal reprimand
- Reparation and Compensation, but no more than two thirds of the youngster's pocket money
- Curtailment of leisure extras
- Additional household chores
- Increased supervision.

Underpinning the Regulations is the philosophy of sound management of the Home, by people in whom the workers have confidence and overall good professional practice and good personal relationships with the youngsters.

This philosophy helps produce practical measures that help make the experience a meaningful one for the youngsters. These include:

Joining in decisions

As youngsters grow up, as part of the development of maturity, they need to take an increasing part in the decisions made about their lives. At 15–16 years of age (the predominant age level) they should be full participants though not necessarily the final deciders. They must feel that their views do really count. This will help reduce tension and a source of potential conflict.

Residents' meetings

These give youngsters a feeling of personal investment in the Home and its routines. It extends to the youngsters joining in decision-making about their own lives to include learning how to co-operate with others, share and compromise to reach a mutually acceptable conclusion. It can prove to be one of their most important, and rewarding, learning experiences.

Problems with interaction can be raised either by the youngsters themselves, or by workers. Where this has been tried in schools, even with 7–8 year olds, bullies have been confronted and so forced to face up to their behaviour by their victims who gain confidence in the shared group setting.

As a by-product workers will be able to assess individual youngsters' interactions and their developing maturity.

Counselling

The youngsters coming into Residential Care frequently have multiple and deep-seated problems which cannot be neglected. Their attitudes to life and to other people, including authority-figures will often stem from poor earlier experiences. They need not only new experiences of caring people but help in dealing with the emotions and the thinking arising from those earlier experiences.

This will call for counselling by workers either in one-to-one sessions (formal or informal) or by group-work. In many cases these will need to be not only behaviour modification programmes but the more direct helping and supporting counselling as the youngsters go through painful re-appraisals and re-adjustments. For some this will need to be accompanied by work to increase their self-confidence.

Consent to rules

When youngsters see that the rules, especially where they have had a part in devising them at Residents Meetings, are not arbitrary but are reasonable and applied fairly, evenly and consistently to all, they are more likely to be accepted by all.

The material condition of the Home

These should be made good as quickly as possible after any damage has been caused. Once the conditions are allowed to deteriorate, they are likely to go downhill with increasing rapidity. If the youngsters can take a pride in their Home, they are more likely not to vandalise it. Especially if they have had a hand in decorating it.

Staffing ratios

These must be high enough to cope with the youngsters' demands on their time and attention. For a youngster to be brushed off at a point they want to talk, perhaps for the first time meaningfully, may cause a reaction that seems out of all proportion to the event. But workers can only spread their attention so far and other matters may be more pressing. So there needs to be enough workers to meet the need.

Secure accommodation

Secure Accommodation has to be specifically approved by the Secretary of State for this use because it removes the liberty of the youngsters to leave such premises. They are governed by the Children (Secure Accommodation) Regulations 1991 and are intended for:

- Those charged with, or convicted of, an imprisonable offence carrying a sentence of fourteen years or more
- Those charged with, or convicted of, an offence of violence
- Those detained under Section 53 of the Children Act 1989
- Those for whom it is the only way of responding to the likelihood of their coming to 'significant harm' or likelihood of injuring themselves or others.

The premises must be 'safe and secure' and periods of residence are time-limited under the Regulations.

Those youngsters falling within the last category are those for whom the Secure Accommodation is seen as the last resort of the Community Care system, when everything else has been tried and failed. Youngsters are not to be sent there for or as punishment but on the basis that a period of residence there is necessary for their welfare, which is the paramount consideration. The decision to place a youngster in Secure Accommodation should be made at Senior Management level and be part of an overall care-plan and is to be used only as long as necessary in each case.

The workers for this type of Accommodation must be selected for their skills at dealing with difficult youngsters, and staffing ratios must be enhanced to give them time to deal with them.

Special programmes have been provided to help them with this.

Safety and security

Workers in all kinds of Residential establishments (not only Community Homes for youngsters) are in a position where the clients have contact with them on the workers' territory, but at the same time most of that territory is also the clients' home (as far as it can be). A Residential worker has an authority greater than any Field worker who is seeing clients whether in his/her own office or in the client's home.

That authority, when accepted by a youngster, is a powerful control. But with a youngster who is very anti-authority it may still not be sufficient.

In a Residential Home there should always be at least double-cover so that workers are available to defuse situations before they become critical, as well as to allow them to be available for on-going work with the residents, especially if they are youngsters.

After a problem situation between a worker and youngster, in most circumstances they will both remain in the Home. This is advantageous because the youngster will see that a relationship is not necessarily destroyed by a piece of bad behaviour and the worker will be able to make more moves to resolving the underlying problem. However, in some circumstances, it may be necessary to move the youngster out to another Home.

The Officer-in-Charge will need to bear in mind the possibility of aggression and violence being shown to workers by youngsters, either singly or in groups, against one worker or against all who are on duty at a particular point of time.

Pre-emptive action on two levels can be taken:

General action

This includes the creation of a good atmosphere in the Home that the newcomers move into; where there is a general assumption that there will be good relationships between the youngsters and workers. The newcomer should be given a welcome – a shared drink and cakes, or biscuits if it is not too near a mealtime, can help – be shown around, taken to his/her room by a sympathetic worker and have the Rules (as few as reasonably possible) explained as they go. Youngsters of this age will be put off by a written list being pushed into their hands with an instruction to read and abide by them. However, there should be a list in their rooms to which they can refer.

Introductions to other youngsters on the way can help more, and if possible and appropriate, one could be asked, at the end of the formal session, to tell the newcomer about the TV, library, games-room etc. This gives the newcomer someone else of the same approximate age to start his/her time with.

If there is a 'key worker' system in the Home, which there really should be, that should be explained, and the name given. This introduction should be made at the earliest opportunity, ideally the key worker should be on duty when the youngster arrives and will do the showing round.

As soon as possible, discussions between the worker and young-ster at a level appropriate to his/her age and level of ability should commence about his/her personal programme. Aspects to be covered include the reasons s/he has been moved there, details of what will happen next together with any other objectives.

This kind of introduction will bring the newcomer into a warm atmosphere with a first impression of caring people who have expectations of him/her, which will help to reduce any anxiety and tension or consequent withdrawal or aggressiveness which can so often accompany a new admission.

These principles apply to all types of establishments whether ordinary residential Homes, Support Units or Secure Accommoda-tion.

Specific action

Workers need to accept that aggression and violence at various levels may occur with the youngsters and that all the principles described earlier apply in Residential Homes just as they do in field offices (see chapter 3) or on Home visits (see chapter 4). So without becoming over-anxious, workers will need to watch for signs that tensions are growing which might lead to a degree of violence between the youngsters themselves or against the workers.

In this type of group setting the Closing Options Concept (see chapter 4) is particularly relevant. By intervening swiftly but appropriately a developing situation can be defused before a real problem arises. But when it does arise, workers will need to assess the problem accurately and the reasons for it erupting.

Youngsters are capable of rapid changes in their styles of behaviour but by the time they are 15–16 years old they have frequently built-up consistent patterns of conduct and responses – essentially, Baseline behaviour (see chapter 1). So, especially for that age group, workers need to be aware not only of the youngster's personal and family history but as much of their Baseline behaviour as possible.

This should not be confined to the Home's Manager alone but

should be known to the workers who have the closer dealings with the youngster and having to immediately cope with his/her behaviour.

Case study

In a Home late one night, the youngsters decided to rush around the place, creating noise and mayhem, so pressurising the workers to chase around after them to quell the noise and disruption. The youngsters loved it! In the debriefing session the reasons for the youngsters behaviour was analysed. The Manager, as an alternative strategy, suggested that if or when, it happened again the workers should make a pot of tea, sit in chairs in one of the main corridors so that they would be seen by the youngsters – and just chat among themselves, thus ignoring the youngsters. By doing this they would not be joining in the game for which the youngsters set them up.

It did happen again. The workers adopted the alternative strategy. Within a very short time the youngsters stopped their rampaging about and came to see why the workers were not chasing about after them as they had planned. They were disconcerted that the workers were not playing their game. And the behaviour stopped.

A similar technique was adopted when a youngster physically challenged a worker. The worker calmly announced, 'I am not playing that kind of game with you,' and walked away.

Perhaps most youngsters will react to frustration by acceptance, or perhaps sulking, shouting or gesturing. But there are youngsters who will react very violently to minor frustrations, and very occasionally a level of violence may lie within his/her parameters of acceptability that would generally be regarded as abnormal in its degree and ferocity.

But there is a major problem in this; a youngster who has developed a certain pattern of responses to one set of circumstances and situations, is labelled to such a degree that style of response is always expected by everyone to any set of circumstances and all situations. That is not only unfair to the youngster him/herself, but is likely to reinforce the poor image s/he may have of him/herself rather than to encourage him/her to change response patterns.

The delicate balance is perhaps best made where the workers are aware of the youngster's previous responses, which *may* be repeated in other circumstances and situations, and are aware that they will not *necessarily* be repeated.

It was well put in 'Control and Discipline in Community Homes' (DHSS Working Party Jan. 1991). 'The unavoidable difficulties which
arise will be best dealt with by staff exercising their own judgement, within a framework of clear policies and planned procedures.'

13 Hostels: statutory and Voluntary

Social Service Departments provide a wide range of homes and hostels for specialist needs groups such as the elderly, the disabled and those with learning difficulties. And there is a large range of voluntary bodies that cater for those groups as well. Although sometimes difficulties of aggression and even violence, perhaps from frustration at their own disabilities, occur in these homes, they are not included in this analysis. However, the same principles of pre-emptive action, awareness and dealing with parallel situations apply even though the clientele is very different.

The term 'Hostels' usually covers a wide range of provisions including ordinary lodging houses and multiple bed-sit accommodation which often caters for similar people to Personal Service clients, or indeed people who are clients. The term is used here to mean accommodation that is non-commercial, where there is some kind of Warden supervision even if it is non-residential and where there is intended to be some element of Social Work help available.

Voluntary Hostels

In most conurbations there are Emergency Shelters which will allow limited-period stays only, often ranging from 3–5 nights. They are basic and cheap and will offer help and advice, especially on how to move on to more settled accommodation.

Short-stay Hostels are for longer period stays than Emergency Shelters offer. They are not permanent homes although they usually have no fixed time limit. The range of standards and facilities offered is great and a client can move on through this system, steadily improving his/her standard of living. Some are shared accommodation but are there more single room situations developing with shared kitchen and bathroom. Sometimes full or half-board is offered, others are self-catering. They are clearly a move-on facility and clients would usually be expected to go from there into the settled commercially rented, local authority or Housing Association accommodation with fully independent living.

'Voluntary' refers to the fact that they are managed by independent committees which may receive much of their income from the Home Office (e.g. when they make beds available for Probation clients or ex-prisoners), the Department of Social Security or local authorities. People may reside there voluntarily or sometimes under a Bail Order from the court or as a Condition of a Probation order.

Statutory Hostels

Throughout the UK there are 112 Bail and Probation Hostels, many of them offering the two functions. Some have 'cluster' houses accommodating clients regarded as more mature around the 'core' hostel building. The cluster buildings are not necessarily next door to the core hostel but do need to be fairly close for the degree of supervision that is still necessary.

Bail Hostels

These are usually short-stay, although the legal process can mean a client going to Crown Court may be there some considerable time. They are regarded as being an alternative to a remand in prison. Most clients are young adults rather than middle-aged or elderly, although there are such clients. They are usually homeless with several, perhaps many, previous convictions and are often volatile. They may have problems of drug or alcohol abuse and sometimes still use solvents.

Regimes are generally relaxed within the minimum requirements set by the Bail Conditions and the rules of the Hostel. Should the Resident Breach the Conditions or the rules, the Bail place is withdrawn and the Resident goes back to Court for Breach.

Probation hostels

These are longer stay where the Residents live under a Condition of a
Probation Order (a Condition of Residence). Almost invariably the
clients have stayed there for a period of assessment on Bail and have
been considered suitable to stay there and the client has agreed to the
Condition being inserted into the Probation Order. Breach of the
Hostel rules can mean s/he goes back to Court for Breach of Probation
Order Requirements.

Resettlement Units

There are nineteen Resettlement Units run by the Department of
Social Security throughout the UK, almost all in or near conurbations. Originating from the workhouses, they received a new title of
'Part III Accommodation' under the National Assistance Act 1948.
Now few in number, they offer basic accommodation to the homeless
of over eighteen years of age. The main client group, however, tends
to be considerably older than that. The objective of Resettlement
Units is to assist the homeless to resettle (hence their title) to a more
stable way of life and often have a progression of accommodation on
one site, with links to outside Agencies whom the Residents can move
onto from the Unit itself.

The clients

The clients of Hostels do vary somewhat in their origins and
backgrounds, but there are some common factors which intensify as
they age.

Family breakdown

As youngsters in local authority residential establishments have
experienced family breakdown, the primary reason they are there, so
too have clients of Hostels. But because these residents are older the
family breakdown will have been longer and maybe deeper and so
reconciliation is harder to achieve.

Homelessness

This is an inevitable consequence of family breakdown until, or
unless, the homeless person can find an environment in which s/he can
develop a stable lifestyle.

Rootlessness

As the homeless drift they have no place, with which they can identify at any personal level, which is smaller than a town. Nor do they have people closer than a loose collection of acquaintances with whom they can group but not usually develop deep relationships. A factor to be borne in mind is that such people have often learned to distrust making deeper relationships because their experience has taught them that they are likely to be betrayed. Consequently their feelings of loneliness and isolation increase unless they find a way to break the cycle.

Inevitably a lack of feeling for others develops and a tendency to live for their own immediate situation.

Abuse problems

A high proportion of Hostel clients have, or are developing, alcohol or drug addictions and some will still be 'hooked' on solvent abuse. This will increase the unpredictability of their behaviour both at normal times and when they are 'high'.

Aggression and violence

Given the mixed backgrounds of residents in Hostels, there is always likely to be an element of aggression and potential violence. People who were 'difficult' in Care are likely to have graduated to Hostel living – which is not dissimilar to what they were used to. Lessons learned in past years are used in the present situation. Attitudes to fellow residents and workers adopted when in Care will be continued now.

But now the residents are physically bigger and stronger, their behaviour may be more volatile and outlook more aggressive. When coupled with the effects of substance abuse, their behaviour can be erratic and unpredictable.

Other residents will be out of their depth if their alleged offences have caused the family break-up, such as incest cases, especially as they will be older than most experiencing a similar situation.

Hostel life

A person new to Hostel life needs to be brought into the existing group of workers and residents. A warm welcome can be given even while the necessary documentation is gone through, especially if the period of residence is a result of a Court Order. For these age groups a clear explanation of the rules of the Hostel (still as few as reasonably possible) are gone through, a copy given to him/her and a copy signed by the new resident is put in his/her file. This will be needed if Breach action becomes necessary. A cup of coffee is useful in making this a less formal occasion. It can be more relaxed without losing its significance.

S/he should then be shown round the Hostel, to his/her room and introduced to any other residents who are around.

Many Hostels in the Voluntary sector have residents who are not on any form of Statutory order. They will still need to have the rules explained to them but clearly this will be more informal. Setting the boundaries is still important, as it is in any landlord–tenant relationship.

Residents meetings

A number of longer stay Hostels, especially the therapeutic centres, have regular residents meetings to discuss matters relevant to the functioning of the Hostel. These are seen as being different from, and additional to, any therapeutic groups. Topics covered include the development of Hostel facilities, the routines of the Hostel, and quite frequently deal with applications for admission. They are the forum for raising complaints or for making suggestions generally.

The philosophy behind the meetings is that the residents are the clients or customers of the Hostel facilities which thereby confers the right to have a voice in its running. It also helps create an atmosphere of personal involvement and so 'ownership' of the Hostel, its facilities and routines. As new clients arrive they are brought into that atmosphere and so the tradition is maintained and thereby the potential for violent action is reduced.

Problems can arise though, if a group of clients hi-jacks the meeting and try to push through proposals that are unacceptable to the managers, or the Hostel's Management Committee.

It would therefore be wise for the rules of the residents meeting to have built into them the reserve that the Management have the final decision, perhaps vested in the Management Committee.

Clearly, for the meeting to have the effect that is wanted the residents must feel, and see, that their views are effective in influencing things.

The hostel areas

All Residential establishments have the same four areas where the needs of security and staff safety differ from each other: these are the Office, the Domestic Area, the Shared Areas and the Personal. The degree of security of each will vary according to the Hostel and type of client normally accepted. In a Hostel that is a bed-sit with the landlord–tenant system and social work support available if needed, any security would only be needed for the office – if there is one. The kitchen would necessarily be open. On the other hand an Emergency Shelter may need a considerably higher degree all round.

In all Statutory Hostels, and Hostels taking Statutory clients it would be advisable for the Domestic area to be secured as well. As such, clients are either alleged offenders on remand or convicted offenders, probably including those involved in violence or weapons offences. It is clearly appropriate that ready access to the kitchens, where potential weapons such as knives are stored, should not be available. If it were always open and a dispute between residents erupted, they would probably make a dash for the kitchen!

There is a delicate balance to be made when deciding on the degree of supervision in the Shared Areas such as the Pool Room or TV Lounge. This needs to be judged not only on the type of resident currently in the Hostel but on an almost hour-by-hour assessment. A worker drifting into the Pool Room upon hearing raised voices, or simply because s/he notices a certain resident going in when there is already another resident there with whom s/he has a dispute, can defuse a possible confrontation, or enable him/her to intervene to prevent an explosion. However, neither workers nor residents would want the situation to be one where the worker is constantly on watch, as in a prison.

An even more careful balancing act is needed over the degree of privacy accorded to the Resident's Personal room or cupboard. Should the room ever be searched? Should the Resident be asked to empty the cupboard or drawers for the contents to be checked? Is the Resident totally trusted not to conceal alcohol, drugs, weapons or stolen goods in his/her own room?

If there is a checking policy then that must be clearly explained in the rules and only undertaken in the presence of the resident. If they are done in his/her absence intense resentment will be caused and, if any contraband is found, will cause accusations of the workers 'planting' it.

Response to violence

An adult Hostel has marked differences to Childrens' Residential establishments. A non-Statutory resident can be ordered to leave it at once or on notice, and the police be called to assist in his/her eviction. A Resident on a Statutory Order cannot be evicted in the same way, but can be arrested and removed by the police for either Breach of Bail or Breach of a Condition of a Probation Order or Licence.

These are the ultimate sanctions. But they don't deal with the situation while the police are coming, unless a warning about them is sufficient to quieten the situation.

The measures described so far in earlier Chapters are as applicable to problems in a Hostel as elsewhere.

In a Hostel particularly, a distinction must be drawn between a brief incident and one that is more protracted. Different action from the worker is needed.

Violence against property

An incident where a kick breaks a table leg and is then over, needs to be treated differently from when a resident begins to completely wreck a room. In the former case the resident can be taken aside and the reasons for the outburst discovered and the matter resolved.

But should a worker intervene to stop the room being wrecked? Certainly an attempt to stop it verbally should be made. To physically intervene by grabbing the resident in a Restraint hold will depend on what training the worker has had, whether in wrecking the room the resident now has a broken chair or table leg in his/her hand ready to use on the worker if s/he moves in, and the relative capabilities of the resident and worker.

It may be that a quick telephone call to the police to arrest the resident is more appropriate when verbal attempts fail.

A basic principle is that property is less important than people. A wrecked table is easily repaired or replaced – a wrecked worker isn't!

Resident to resident violence

In this situation the time factor is again important. A swearing match between two residents can be dealt with by a reprimand – such incidents are common between residents.

A single swift push or punch, about which the victim wants no other action taken, can be dealt with by a reprimand and a warning by the workers involved. It may be decided after further discussion that other action might be necessary, if the victim is willing to give evidence and the giving of the reprimand hasn't blocked off that course of action. In either of those two events no further action is possible.

A fight between residents beyond the single punch or push requires different decisions. A worker would undoubtedly be expected to intervene verbally by telling them to stop it and warning them of the consequences, especially if the police are called and they are on a Court Order. If warnings are given, the action must be carried out if the fighting continues. If it isn't, future warnings will have no credibility.

A worker may decide to intervene physically especially if s/he has had training but that must be decided within the policies of the particular Hostel.

Physical intervention may take the form of pulling one away from the other, pushing them away from each other, or getting between them, shouting warnings at them throughout. This carries the obvious danger that one or both residents may turn on the worker, especially if one thinks the worker is aiding the other.

If there are two workers on duty they can each tackle one if that is the Hostel policy.

Resident to worker violence

This may happen in various circumstances:

- when intervening in resident to resident situations
- when interviewing a resident, perhaps telling him/her that an unfavourable Report is being made because of their behaviour
- when trying to control a resident who has come back to the Hostel under the influence of alcohol or drugs.

The response measures for dealing with violent clients in offices also apply in the Hostel setting but that has the added complication that it is highly likely that other residents will be at hand providing an audience for the violent resident to play to and to give added pressure to the worker to respond appropriately and to be right in what s/he does.

Other residents may choose to intervene on the worker's behalf acting as voluntary back-up but it is not good practice to ask them to do so, Complications can arise if they are too enthusiastic in 'restraining' the violent resident. There can be conflicts of loyalty between them, different residents choose different sides and a generalised fight breaks out or the Residents who join in on the worker's side later demand favours in return. They might ask for them anyway if they chose to join in for themselves, but the worker, whilst thanking them for their help will find the request easier to refuse.

There is great advantage in having sufficient workers to provide 'double-cover' at all times. This not only helps provide a sense of security for the workers themselves, but means there are two people to be aware of what the Residents are doing and to provide immediate back-up for each other when the difficult situations arise. This will make it easier to deal with them *in situ* and also mean that there will be another person to telephone for the police should that be necessary.

14 The legal situation

It is important that workers are as fully aware of the law in violence situations, as in any other area of their work.

The law does not give workers in the Personal Services any rights or privileges over and above the ordinary citizens in violence situations. Although workers are dealing with the same types of people as the police do, usually not in identical roles, they have none of the constabulary's powers, responsibilities and protections. For example, none are permitted to carry staves (or truncheons) and handcuffs. When Social Workers go to investigate Child Abuse cases, or cases where allegations are made of ill-treatment of children, they may be accompanied by the police, especially if violent behaviour is expected or anticipated.

Nor is it safe to assume that Courts will necessarily be more sympathetic to workers if they are brought before them on a charge of assault, whether the charges are brought by the Crown Prosecution Service or by a disgruntled client. In fact, the opposite might happen if the Court should adopt the view that it was a case of workers abusing their position.

And the media have no built-in sympathy or support for workers and may, at times, be more ready to accuse them of abuse of their position.

All three measures of dealing with violent clients (break-away, restraint and self-defence) have elements in which the client may get hurt. The only way to break a strangle-hold may be to bend back the little finger of the attacker's hand. And it could be broken. Restraint holds and Self-Defence techniques can also cause injury to the assailant and are more likely to do so.

Defending oneself

The law in this situation, which covers all three groups of techniques, was clearly described in the Appeal Judgement given in Palmer v Regina in 1971 and still applies today. The judge stated, 'It is both good law and common sense that a man who is attacked may defend himself. It is both good law and common sense that he may do, but may only do, what is reasonably necessary. But everything will depend on the particular facts and circumstance.'

The generality of the last sentence gives little precise guidance. The other great variable is the definition of what is seen as 'reasonably necessary' in the judge's preceding sentence. For a judge's view in the quiet and calm of a court room may not be the same as that of a worker embroiled in a violent situation where, at times, assessments and judgements have to be made in split seconds. That may also apply with Senior Managers or a Management Committee in a Disciplinary Hearing.

But in spite of that, there are some indicators that do give some guidance.

- Self-defence is permitted in law
- Self-defence is permitted in law to the extent of what is 'reasonably necessary' to stop that attack
- Self-defence is *not* permitted in law beyond what is 'reasonably necessary' in time and degree to stop the attack.

There is no obligation in Statute law for a person to retreat as far as possible. However, when a Court is considering whether action taken in self-defence was 'reasonably necessary' they are likely to take into account whether the defender made any effort to retreat first. After all, the defender may have been able to get away totally and easily. However, if there was that attempt and retreat was impossible or became impossible for any of a variety of reasons, and the attack was continuing, self-defence action would inevitably be deemed to be 'reasonable'.

But while the judgement showed that it is permissible to use force in self-defence, it also showed that the measures taken must be limited in time and degree to what is commensurate with the threat or attack levels.

The 'time' factor means that self-defence can only last as long as the attack lasts, or the belief that the attack was going to continue. There must be valid grounds for having that belief. If, for example, the former attacker had begun to run away and the former defender hit him on the back of the head, there would be no valid ground for the belief that the attack was going to be continued, and the erstwhile defender becomes the attacker. Retaliation is not self-defence.

The 'degree' factor limits self-defence measures to the level of the attack. For example, if the attacker is using punches, the degree of self-defence of smashing a chair over his/her head would not be regarded as commensurate.

However, that itself is not absolutely rigid.

The test of 'reasonableness' includes *all* the circumstances of the incident, including the defenders own physical condition. So, if an able-bodied attacker attacked a handicapped person who needed to use a walking-stick, if s/he hit the attacker with the walking-stick while the attack was continuing, that would be most probably considered as 'reasonable' in all the circumstances even though the walking stick had been used as a weapon against a weaponless attacker.

Those are the 'objective' factors that would be considered by the court.

To make that already complex situation even more complicated the court will take into account the 'Subjective' factors – what the defender *believed*, on firm and reasonable grounds, the attacker was intending to do to him/her.

For example, if an angry client leaps up from the chair and advances towards the worker with fist upraised and shouting s/he was going to 'batter' the worker, it is reasonable for the worker to believe s/he is about to be attacked.

That would entitle the worker to take Self-Defence action, if retreat is not possible, which could be pre-emptive in that type of situation. It is not possible to generalise as to what action might be considered as 'reasonable' in that situation – there are too many variables. But if taking into account all the circumstances the belief of the defender was 'reasonable' (as in this example it certainly would be), then the plea of 'Self-Defence' would very likely, stand.

Once that plea has been put forward in court then it is up to the prosecution to show that either the defender did *not* have that belief (very difficult) or that the belief itself was 'unreasonable' in all the circumstances.

Defending others

It may happen that the worker when attacked is in a position where escaping would leave other vulnerable people in the room , leave them at the mercy of an aggressive and violent client. If it is the worker who has brought them together, perhaps to try to effect a reconciliation, there is a greater moral, if not legal, responsibility to ensure the safety of all the clients, even from each other.

There is both Statute and Common Law that is relevant:

Statute law

Criminal Law Act 1967 Section 3

'A person may use such force as is reasonable in the circumstances in the prevention of crime or in effecting or assisting in the lawful arrest of offenders or suspected offenders or of persons unlawfully at large.

Police and Criminal Evidence Act 1984 Section 25

'Any person may arrest without warrant anyone who is, or whom he reasonably suspects to be committing an arrestable offence.'

An 'arrestable offence' is one for which the sentence is fixed by law, where the sentence could be five years imprisonment, or any criminal damage, or an indecent assault on a woman.

Common law

Any person may arrest where a breach of the peace is being committed or about to be committed in the immediate future, or is about to be renewed.

A person threatening or attacking another therefore falls within any of these. A worker, intervening to stop such an attack on another is acting in the 'prevention of crime' and 'reasonable force' can be used. Detaining the client until the police arrive to formally arrest and charge, if that is decided upon, is possible under either of the Acts or the Common Law provision.

The common thread throughout is, be aware of what is 'reasonable' in all circumstances. This means that workers in the Personal Services must be able and willing to think ahead, use professional judgement and skills, and to act with common sense should crises develop and violence erupt.